THE NIGER DELTA PARADOX

PARADOX

Impoverished in the Midst of Abundance

THE NIGER DELTA PARADOX

PARADOX

Impoverished in the Midst of Abundance

by

JOHN K. WANGBU

Safari Books Ltd.
Ibadan

Published by
Safari Books Ltd.
Ile Ori Detu 1, Shell Close
Onireke, Ibadan.
Email: safarinigeria@gmail.com
Website: http://safaribooks.com.ng

© 2018, John K. Wangbu
First Published 2018

ISBN: Paperback- 978-978-55986-1-2
Cased- 978-978-55986-2-9

DEDICATION

To:
All Niger Deltans, a people impoverished by their own oil.

TABLE OF CONTENTS

FOREWORD (1)

Any book on the Niger Delta region of Nigeria has a story to tell. Daily, stunning fresh information on neglect and abuse keep emerging. In the same manner, those with little knowledge of the area and the issues have always seen every book on the region as an adventure in protest. In most cases, they are right because it is a protest against pollution of the atmosphere through gas flaring; protest against environmental degradation or destruction through abandoned oil spill sites; protest against human death attributed to inhuman activities of the oil exploring companies; protest against injustice done to the people through the non-payment of statutorily allowed compensations over the destruction of their farmlands and homes among others.

The Niger Delta is a story in contradictions. Described by many researchers as one of the richest regions of the world, the Niger Delta is equally one of the most neglected and impoverished regions of the world. If the word 'neglect' has ever achieved its real meaning or dared to manifest in the physical, the Niger Delta region is a typical example.

A journey through the region is a journey through the Biblical valley of the shadow of death. It is even worse. It is an adventure into the valley of deprivation. The question is: was it always like this? And the answer is an emphatic no! It all started in 1956 when, as the story goes, crude oil was discovered in commercial quantity in Oloibiri. Then things changed. What was seen as a blessing soon became a curse. A people that once lived in peace became a people cursed to death.

As the explorers kept exploring and the exploiters exploited, the environment became a victim. The land that was the source of wealth to the people was drained of nutrients that hitherto made farming a delight. As oil spilled on the farmlands, the land lost its value and importance. The sea and streams that were sources of livelihood to the people soon became the very reason for their poverty as oil spills travelled deep and far, poisoning and killing fishes and everything aquatic.

Those who have not experienced the agony faced by the Niger Delta people would always dismiss their outcry and protest as nothing other than greed. But as captured on the pages of this book, the level of deprivation, destruction and destitution imposed upon the region by the oil companies, the local and national governments require a revisitation. Promises have been made by various governments; wonderful suggestions have been made by the various groups and commissions assigned to look into the issues even from the pre-independent years, still no adequate action has been taken to implement the required solution.

This book by Monsignor John K. Wangbu may not present the final solution to the cries and the crisis of the Niger Delta; but it is a huge contribution towards analytically drawing further attention to the plight of the people and putting in perspectives what could have been done several decades ago to ensure that the Niger Delta recovers from age-long environmental abuse and human injustice.

'TIMI ALAIBE

FOREWORD (II)

Small is beautiful, but such a beauty has its problems. To be a small fish in a big pond is to be in danger of being swallowed by the big fish. To be a minority in a country with major ethnic groups is to be in danger of being swallowed by the big and powerful groups, if minority rights are not respected.

In a democratic system, decisions are made by the majority, based on the general conviction that the judgment of the majority is more likely to be right than that of the minority. But the majority rule does not give a free hand to the majority to do as it wants.

The Niger Delta region, which structures the Nigerian economy, is today a victim of a small fish in a big pond, with the threat to be swallowed. The resources God has put beneath the earth are essentially for the people living there. And so, most of the benefits derived from such natural resources should first go to the people God has prepared that place for. Any arrangement that does not accord priority benefit to the people who are sitting on any type of resources is a deviation from natural justice.

The Niger Delta has historically been a fertile area, and consequently has been important to Nigeria for at least two reasons. Before oil was discovered in commercial quantity in 1956, the Niger Delta region was the major food producing area and was termed the "breadbasket" of the nation. Since 1958, the Niger Delta has been the source of million barrels of crude oil, vital to the Nigerian economy.

Despite the vast resources of our region, the majority of our people are poor, over sixty per cent have no access to primary health care, and unemployment among the educated youth threatens social and political stability.

The Niger Delta region of Nigeria has become a hot bed of troubles, owing to the persistence of environmental challenges dating back to decades of apparent inactivity and negligence by governments and oil industry operators. Today, these challenges have become great threats to the Niger Delta ecosystem and its peoples. The once fertile land has now been polluted with unpardonable oil spillage.

Our country is a composition of majority and minority ethnic groups. Therefore, the content or form of our democracy must not only recognise the equality of persons but also the relevance of cultural units to which each individual citizen has a profound sense of belonging. Our democratic format and behaviour must show sensitivity to the anxiety not only to the majority but equally of the minority ethnic groups. And such sensitivities will need to be accommodated in the constitutions of the state.

Moreover, the world has grown increasingly complex and interdependent. Here lies both the beauty and the danger. Evidences are before us that even a family dispute in an Ogoni village today could affect New York Stock Exchange that will influence business in India. The inter-connectedness of economic life seen in the practice of trade, capital investment, and monetary policy, along with institutions like transnational corporations, all make the isolation of domestic economy from other national economies unlikely.

The reality is becoming more obvious that we live in a world of interconnectedness. Human beings have multiple loyalties: religious, class, ideological ties that prevent individuals from enveloping into ethnic cocoon. Problems of the environment, refugees, or drug trafficking require that multicultural and multiethnic concerns act in patriotic alliance. Although the oil and gas and other resources in the Niger Delta belong primarily to the people of the region, we should be prepared to share with our brothers and sisters from other parts of Nigeria, but not at our expense.

The most important factor in any nation's development is human capital. In this book, Msgr. John K. Wangbu, a Catholic priest and a citizen of Niger Delta discusses one of the best options of addressing the problems of Niger Delta. The beauty of this book is the non-violent and educative option it took in addressing our needs. It was Albert Einstein who once said:

> There is no scientific antidote, only education. You have got to change the way people think. I am not interested in disarmament talks between nations... What I want to do is to disarm the mind. After that, everything else will automatically follow. The ultimate weapon for such mental disbarment is ... education.

The issues discussed in this book are important and timely. In focusing on the many issues of the Niger Delta region: environment, business ethics, minority and human rights and power politics, this book is very remarkable. I highly recommend it to researchers, policy makers, business executives and the general public.

Sir Dr. Peter O. Odili

PREFACE

———•·———

Many people in the Niger Delta may not have heard of the term "environmental injustice" before, but it is just a new word for an old problem. Environmental justice is based on the principle that all people have a right to be protected from environmental pollution and to live in and enjoy a clean and healthful environment. Environmental justice is the equal protection and meaningful involvement of all people with respect to the development, implementation and enforcement of environmental laws, regulations and policies and the equitable distribution of environmental benefits.[1]

It is clear that environmental injustice does exist in the Niger Delta. In the Niger Delta, we experience environmental injustice mostly from the activities of the oil industries which have degraded our land, contaminated our water and polluted the air without proper compensation. Gas leakage is killing many people and continues to have a negative impact on the lives of the people living around the area. This is a well-known example of environmental injustice in the Niger Delta among many others.

It is impossible to eradicate all these forms of injustice all of a sudden, but it must be acknowledged that something has to be done regarding this in the future. Local authorities must be aware of these issues and the probable consequences they may have in the near future. Local authorities must take it as their responsibility to deal with environmental injustice at the grass-roots level. Ignoring and neglecting these issues may not have any direct effects immediately, but it can have future repercussions.

---

1   "Commonwealth of Massachusetts" 2002, 2.

So what can we do to prevent environmental injustice and to bring about true environmental justice? The first thing would be to make ourselves aware of the issues of environmental injustice facing the Niger Delta today. After that, we need to get involved.

Environmental justice in the Niger Delta found its pioneer voice in Ken Saro-Wiwa who tried to address environmental issues in the region. This book is my modest contribution to environmental justice.

ACKNOWLEDGEMENTS

Writing an acknowledgement is indeed the most difficult task in book writing. When I remember the people who have not only been instrumental in my embarking on this project, but also all the people who have been my benefactors and believed in me over the years, and enabled me to even get to this point of my life, I get overwhelmed with the unquantifiable love and benevolence I have been shown. It is therefore difficult to acknowledge all the individuals who have touched my life in various ways knowingly or unknowingly. To do so would be to write another book.

Are you one of those who have ever been kind to me, said encouraging words to me, advised and helped me in some way, taught me and prayed for me...? Know that I am ever grateful. Please accept my immense gratitude.

I am deeply thankful to the following: my friend, the Very Rev. Fr. Kekong Bisong, a former colleague at St. Joseph Major Seminary Ikot Ekpene for his wisdom, support and competence. His brilliant guidance and editing have made all the difference and have provided me with the necessary encouragement in writing this book. Fr. Kekong alongside other scholars was a foundation collaborator in my earlier edited book *Niger Delta: Rich Region, Poor People* which is now being developed into a full book. He read this book from the beginning and offered insights. To Dr. Joy Agumagu, I am also grateful. I am grateful to Timi Alaibe for accepting to write the foreword to this book, and providing insights into what life is truly all about for the people of Niger Delta region. The family of Paul Wesiah, Rhode Island, United States of America who were there when I needed them, especially during my turbulent 2015 Christmas Winter are amazing. I thank Barr. Maxwell Onuah and his wife Barr.

Anne who read portions of the book and offered insights. I wish to also thank Michael Tunde who offered his valuable time in typing and working on sequence of sections.

I acknowledge my bishop, Most Rev. Camillus A. Etokudoh, the chief shepherd of Port Harcourt Catholic Diocese. I will like to honour and thank Rt. Hon. Rotimi Chibuike Amaechi, a dogged fighter for justice and elimination of poverty in the Niger Delta as Governor of Rivers State, Nigeria and even as Federal Minister of Transportation, for his boldness and political astuteness.

I cannot conclude this acknowledgement without thanking my immediate family for their invaluable, ongoing support during difficult moments.

JOHN K. WANGBU

1

INTRODUCTION

Oil companies cannot choose where oil may be found, geology dictates this for them.[2] In Nigeria, oil is found in the Niger Delta. Oil exploration in the Niger Delta region began in 1956, after a long search for oil which began in 1906. The Niger Delta has the third largest mangrove forest in the world, and the largest in Africa. Mangrove forests are important for sustaining local communities because of the ecological functions they perform and the many essential resources they provide, including soil stability, medicines, healthy fisheries, wood for fuel and shelter and critical wildlife habitats.

Unfortunately, oil spills are contaminating, degrading, and destroying mangrove forests. Gas flaring has been the most constant cause of environmental damage in the Niger Delta region. In many places, it has been going on 24 hours a day for over 50 years. The Worldwide Fund for Nature has calculated gas-flaring activities in Nigeria as a major contributor to global warming. Because of nearly six decades of oil extraction, the Niger Delta coastal rainforest and mangrove habitats have become one of the most endangered deltas in the world.

Due to lack of responsibility for the environment, the once fertile farmland has been laid waste by constant oil spills and acid rain. Most spills are caused by such factors as equipment failure and corrosion. Whenever the oil companies accept

---

2   G. CHANDLER, "Oil Companies and Human Rights" *A European Review*, 7, 2., (1989) 69-73, 69.

liability for oil spills, they only pay 'compensation' for surface rights (like farm crops) and not for the land itself. Meanwhile, the people continue to suffer huge and untold losses. Apart from the health risks to which they are exposed by pollution, they suffer losses of economic activities. Fishing activity suffers as fish die from pollution or migrate elsewhere. Farmers are dislodged from the soil they have been using for so many years and all of these losses are not adequately addressed by either the compensation paid or the system of paying.

The flaring of gas that causes some of these difficulties in the Niger Delta is a human rights, environmental and economic atrocity. Many of the oil companies' operations and materials in the region are outdated, in poor condition and would be illegal in other parts of the world. Many pipelines pass within meters from people's homes. As the rural environments are polluted and lack the basic amenities like drinkable water and electricity, the population live in centres of poverty and social discrimination.

The Niger Delta crisis has a long history. It is a long story of dashed hopes and expectations. The crisis that has now engulfed the Niger Delta region began soon after the 1963 Constitution which recognised 50 per cent derivation principle that was amended and it was not long before resources that should have been used for the overall development of the region were diverted to other uses.

While the people of Niger Delta bear the pains of exploitation, the central government controls the resources. This is one of the contentious issues among legal experts. Some maintain that the constitution asserts that the revenue accruing from derivation should go to the communities which sustained losses through the harms of oil extraction.

The construction of a new federal capital territory in Abuja is one of the things that woke up the people of the region to the realisation that they were being short-changed. This discovery was in 1998, when elders and youth leaders in the Niger Delta region were invited to the infamous two-million-man-march rally in Abuja to woo the late Head of State, Gen. Sani Abacha to run for the presidency. When the delegates from the constituent states of the Niger Delta "saw the glittering and impressive level of development in Abuja, they were momentarily thrown into a state of bewilderment." Shocked at the level of development in Abuja, they became angry that their God-given wealth was being used to develop other regions while they suffer. As soon as the boys who went to Abuja returned, they started pressing for better development in the Niger Delta region. Since then, the Niger Delta lost its innocence; the innocence of a rich region impoverished in the midst of abundance.

2

BEFORE NOW

Creation stories vary from one area of the Niger Delta to another. In emphasis, however, they contain the same basic elements: the creative beings are responsible for the features of the land and the entire natural world including the species and plant life. They created the whole world including the species, landform, water. And so, all of these have special sacred meanings, and they continue to be imbued with their life force and interconnectedness. These creative acts took place over a period of time but the creator spirits existed before this work and continue to live in forms that are visible only to those with the ability to see them.

Creator spirits, in bringing all things to life, taught the people they created how they were related to the animate and inanimate world around them, and to the spirits themselves. These relationships are ones of custodianship and responsibility, including ceremony. We are the human elements of the world. If the inhabitants of this world continue to desecrate the universe, then the universe will no longer be a life-giving force.

In the Ikwerre culture, customs, ethos, religious rites, legends, myths, songs, food as well as medicinal purposes are deeply associated with the environment. The Ikwerre culture has a cosmic belief for everything happening in their life, including health and suffering. In the Ikwerre culture, "Mother Earth" is depicted as a living person. The spirit in Ikwerre people is very strong.[3]

In the Ikwerre cosmology, the Earth goddess (*Ali*) is the guardian of morality and any moral infraction (*nso Ali*) against it is visited with sickness or even death.[4]

Actions that are taboo to Ali include homicide, incest, suicide, stealing, sex in the bush, et cetera. They constitute a pollution of the land (*Ali*); and require an elaborate placatory rites by *nye-kwali* (the Chief priest of *Ali*) in order to restore the ritual purity of the community.[5]

Traditionally, the Ikwerre people have exemplified the qualities of good stewardship in their interactions with the environment. Ikwerre environmental knowledge developed over centuries of observing and understanding seasonal changes; changes that were taken into consideration as a natural part of daily life and decision making. Decisions were made with regard to the environment, which ultimately met the needs of individuals, families and communities.

Agriculture was an important and constant practice among the Ikwerre people. As food gatherers, they moved to areas where the land was bountiful,[6] and had a special time to hunt and trap animals for food and clothing, a time to catch fish, to harvest fruits and a time to pick and prepare medicines and roots. In conducting these activities, Ikwerre people considered the growth, reproduction, and regeneration cycles of plants, animals and birds. Actions interrupting these natural cycles and patterns

---

3   Amadi, E. & Wotogbe-Weneka,W "Divinities and Their Roles in Ikwerre Religion and Culture" in Nduka, O. ed, *Studies in Ikwerre History and Culture, Vol. 1* Ibadan , Kraft Books Limited, 94-104.

4   *Olumati Rowland, ibid.*

5   Olumati Rowland, "The Impact of Christianity and Modernity on Ali - Earth Goddess of the Traditional Religion of the Ikwerre People, Rivers State" *in African Research Review,* AFRREV, VOL. 9 (1), S/No 36, January, 2015.

6   Tasie, A. C. M, *Ikwerre Land History, Culture and People* (Port Harcourt: Purity Press Publishers, 2008),

were considered to be acts against the laws of nature. This knowledge and understanding of the natural environment reflected the importance of sustaining Mother Earth for generations to come.

Our culture preached that all constituents of our ambient nature are interrelated. The environment is one and God has bestowed certain powers to certain plains, mountains, forests, rivers and lands which play important roles in the prosperous relationship of human beings. Our ancestors respected the environment and understood relationships between nature and themselves. For centuries, they experimented with the types of crops growing on their lands.

The traditional worship practices show the symbiotic relation of human beings and nature. Our ancestors lived in harmony with nature and conserved its valuable biodiversity. Plants were treated with awe because of their vital roles in human welfare. Plants were valued as nutritional, economic, commercial and medicinal resources. Our ancestors used plants in various ways including worshipping gods and goddesses for the protection and betterment of human life. This is different but serves the same purpose with what our contemporary ecologists are now trying to do; to see the interconnectedness of the natural world. More specifically, to see human beings not as rulers of the earth but as fellow citizens, acknowledging both the living and non-living parts of the environment. All of these were appreciated by our Ikwerre ancestors even when they did not articulate their basic beliefs. For our ancestors, the entire method of living is inherently ecological because, for them, everything in the natural world was interrelated and shared the same life. Their lifestyles as well as their religion only served to emphasise this relationship between humans and their environment.

The Niger Delta before oil

The relationship between our ancestors and their environment cannot, however, be overstated. They paid more attention to their environment because nature, to them, stood for a representation of the sacred. Their religious ceremonies centred around hunting, fishing and cultivation of land for agricultural purposes. They included numerous ceremonies and rituals in their way of life and showed respect for everything they killed. There is an abundance of evidence to show that the traditional hunting of animals and fishing took place within the context of respect because even animals and the fish were understood as being sacred, and hunting and fishing were understood as sacred occupations. These activities were undertaken as religious responsibilities.

A large number of rituals and rules concerning the treatment of animals attest to the fact that in the Ikwerre culture, hunting is as much a religious pursuit as a practical one. Central to the idea that hunting is a sacred occupation is the idea that animals, like human beings, are conscious, social, powerful, spiritual beings that must be approached in respectful ways. Disrespecting these animals result in an unsuccessful hunt as well as poor relationship with the sacred. Animals had to be treated properly because they could represent spirits. The plants were sacred and could give evidence of the supernatural and the land which could reveal the divine.

If we describe our ancestors as ecologists, we do so because they did not waste or despoil, exhaust or extinguish the environment. If an area lacks sufficient adult animals, hunters would leave the area long enough to allow the young populations to develop. Care of hunted animals was also important because our ancestors believed in animal spirits. These animal spirits could be easily upset if proper precautions were not made and would leave the area permanently.

In general, our Ikwerre ancestors attempted, to some extent, to treat every place as if it were sacred. A key theme in their religion is the understanding of hunting as a reciprocal relationship between the hunter and the hunted. Thinking about a successful hunt as primarily the receiving of a gift puts the emphasis, not on the actions and skill of the hunter, but on the violation of the animal that is killed. To give thanks for such a favour, the hunter in return reciprocates by observing a series of ritual gestures that communicate his respect and gratitude to the animal. The act of hunting itself involves a reciprocal obligation for hunters to provide the conditions in which animals can grow and survive on the earth. They also believe that human beings and animals are in communication with each other on a more or less friendly basis under normal conditions. The Ikwerre culture and religions, like most ancestral religions, were to some extent rooted in the environment. Every stream, tree, and mountain contained a guardian spirit who had to be carefully appeased before one put a mill to a stream, or cut a tree, or mined the mountain.

With the discovery of crude oil in the Niger Delta, there was a conscious effort to demystify nature, removing nature spirits and leaving the land devoid of spirit or importance. From then on, the land and natural resources, especially the crude oil was seen as something that human beings could take advantage of and exploit to fit their own needs. From then on, the land was simply regarded as the stage on which humanity carried out its will.

Ecologists know that change is inevitable and can, in some cases, improve the environment as a whole. But given the current circumstances, the world must make conscious and sufficient efforts to save the Niger Delta region from an imminent environmental disaster.

The Ikwerre people and their communities have a vital role to play in the present environmental management of the Niger Delta. The state and the people of the Niger Delta have to collaborate as responsible stakeholders. This is what we refer to as *Ogbaknor*. In Ikwerre, *Ogbaknor* refers to the gathering of villagers, brought together by a common necessity to discuss in public forum the problems of the community. The government of the day should recognise and fully support their identity, culture and interests, and facilitate their effective participation in the achievement of sustainable development. It is necessary for everyone to embrace the concept of survival of the next generations, which is truly the heart of sustainability. We must make decisions that ensure an equitable quality of life for all for generations to come.

Embedded within the Ikwerre worldview is the concept of collective responsibility for tending the land and using only that which is needed for sustenance. Important, as well, is the interconnectedness and interdependence of all life forms: humankind, flora and fauna, and all that exist on the earth. The concept of sustainability is not new to the Ikwerre people; they are very much aware of the growing need for all humans to show greater respect for the environment – respect for Mother Earth if we are to continue to coexist in this world.

Many Ikwerre people embrace sustainability beliefs through their traditional practices. This is evident in the richness and vastness of Ikwerre cultural practices, in particular, the many feasts and celebrations that are held to give thanks for life. There is a celebration and acknowledgement for each season and, as in the past, there is a special time to say "thank you" to the Creator for life.

In a world where sustainability has not been the norm, the challenge for sustainability can be difficult. The Ikwerre people face a double challenge: to maintain their traditional sustainability practices and to achieve equity in a fast-changing world. The Ikwerre perspectives, with respect to traditional environmental knowledge as well as sustainability concepts, can be integrated into educational curricula in order to help teachers and students understand the importance of education towards a sustainable society.

For the multinational oil companies, land owners might consider land as something they own, a commodity to be bought and sold, an asset to make profit from. For the Ikwerre people, the relationship is much deeper. It is the land that owns everybody. It is our Mother Earth and all aspects of our lives are connected to it. We have a profound spiritual connection to land. The Ikwerre law and spirituality are intertwined with the land, the people and creation, and this forms our culture and sovereignty. The health of land and water is central to our culture. Land, as our mother, is steeped in our culture, and also gives us the responsibility to care for it. The land sustains Ikwerre lives in every aspect:

spiritually, physically, socially and culturally. The Ikwerre law and life originate in and are governed by the land. The connection to land gives the Ikwerre people their identity and a sense of belonging.

3

NIGER DELTA

The geographical region that constitutes the Niger Delta extends from the Mahin Creek to the Bight of Benin and from Apoi to Bakkassi. It covers 560 kilometres, which is about 75 per cent of the entire coastline of Nigeria. Covering about 70,000 square kilometres, over half of the region's topography is criss-crossed with creeks and dotted with small islands and the rest has uplands located in the third course, the Niger River; the Delta drains the river into the Atlantic Ocean. Its deltaic soil accounts largely for the huge deposits of oil and gas found in the region. The Niger Delta is said to be the third largest wetland in the world, with fresh, brackish water and mangrove swamp forests. The region is rich in other natural resources, like palm oil, herbal plants, fish, reptiles, and monkeys, among others. The major economic activities of the people are farming and fishing. The most common mode of transportation is by water.

Before the Europeans became interested in the Niger Delta, there were the Ikwerre, Ijaw, Kalabari, Benin, Efik, Annang, Ibibio and hundreds of other ethnic groups or sub-ethnic groups, each with its own cultural heritage, sharing a common ancestry, mythology, homeland, language or dialect.

Niger Delta as a region derives its name from being situated at the mouth of the River Niger. "Delta" is the fourth letter of the Greek alphabet. But the word "delta" has come to mean a piece of land shaped like a triangle that

13

is formed when a river splits into smaller rivers before it flows into an ocean. In 1914, Flora Shaw, later Flora Lugard, the wife of the first Governor General of the amalgamated Nigeria, named the areas that fell within the Muurish Sokoto Emirate and Muurish Benin, *Niger Area*. From *Niger Area*, the name Nigeria was coined. The word "Niger" means river. *N'jer*[7] is the Tamazight's (in Morroco) word for any river.

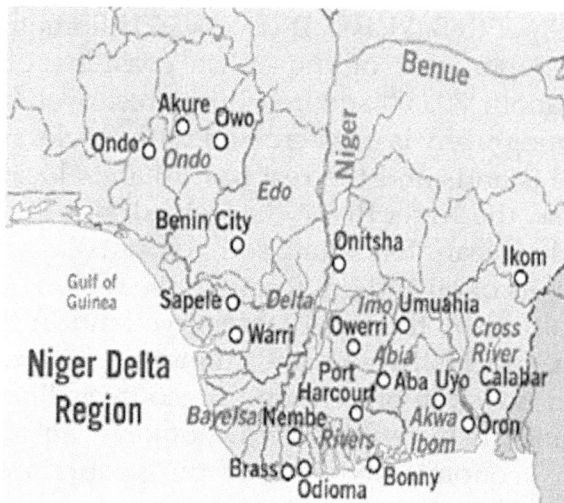

The Niger Delta region

The Mangroves of the Niger Delta

The Niger Delta people have their lands near the delta of the River Niger in the South-South of Nigeria. The delta as a coastline is at the edge or margin of land next to the sea or ocean. The Niger Delta region is made of mangroves which are coastal forests that lie on the crossroad where the ocean's freshwater and land realms meet. They are among

---

7   Kekong Bisong, "Challenges of Niger Delta Oil Based Conflict", in *Wisdom Journal of Theology and Philosophy vol. 2, No.4*

the most productive and complex ecosystems on the planet. The capacity of mangroves to protect against storms and even sea level rise make them indispensable for coastal communities in their fight against climate change.

The mangroves of the Niger Delta are at the interface of land and sea. The mangrove forest forms an ecosystem that attracts a combination of terrestrial, freshwater, estuarine and marine species from the surrounding areas. These species use different parts of mangroves as habitat, including the canopy and branches. Many species of birds and insects can be found within the mangrove canopy. A wide range of mammal species also use the mangroves, including deer, bats and monkeys. Mangroves also harbour a variety of reptiles including snakes, crocodiles and lizards, such as the estuarine crocodile and the mangrove monitor lizard.

The mangrove roots are covered by a wide variety of attached species, including sponges, oysters and mussels, all of which help to filter the water. Mangroves provide several important functions to animals such as breeding and nesting grounds, nurseries, shelter areas, as well as a feeding habitat. A number of migratory bird species rely on mangrove sites along their migratory routes.

Mangroves in the Niger Delta

15

The people of the Niger Delta are highly dependent on mangrove ecosystem services and therefore suffer when mangroves are degraded. In many places, mangrove fish and shellfish supply the main sources of protein for coastal communities. For some coastal villages in the Niger Delta, the destruction of the mangrove forest has significantly resulted in a number of people sinking in poverty.

Mangroves provide goods in the form of wood for construction, fuel-wood, charcoal, furniture, fish traps, as well as non-timber forest products such as honey, fruits, medicine, wine and palm thatch for roofing. In many coastal communities, these commodities can be the primary source of materials for building, cooking, and subsistence. Mangrove products were harvested for direct consumption or for income through trade and employment. In poor coastal areas, mangroves may represent the only source of fuel wood and construction materials available. Access to mangrove resources can therefore act as an important safety net, allowing people to obtain food even when other income streams fail.

The resistance of mangroves to termites means they are prized for use as building poles, supporting a trade in this product. Mangrove charcoal is among the heaviest charcoals and is the mainstay for cooking fires. The value of mangrove timber is demonstrated by the fact that many coastal communities in the Niger Delta have commercial markets specifically for mangrove wood. The density and rot-resistance of some types of mangrove wood and a corresponding ability to withstand exposure to saltwater is the reason this timber is used in boat-building and often used for construction of docks, fences, and fish traps. The wood of several mangroves has been used as material for homes and other buildings, as well as railroad ties.

Parts of mangrove plants, including leaves, fruits, flowers and roots are used in traditional medicine to treat a range of diseases and ailments including leprosy and tuberculosis. Some of the medications in our local drug stores owe their origin to materials derived from tropical forests. Tropical forests offer hope for anti-cancer drugs and compounds for coronary disorders. Trees have been used as treatment against malaria since time immemorial. Destruction of these forests leads to destruction of medicinal plants that could be used as treatment for various ailments.

The palm tree provides an important source of thatch and is also used to make syrup, juice, wine and vinegar.[8] Mangrove honey – with its subtle sweetness and tinge of saltiness – is a valuable commodity in coastal communities. Local sales of handicrafts made from mangrove can supplement a household's income in many marginalised communities.

A large number of fish species utilise mangroves during all or part of their lives, with the mangrove providing critical food, shelter and refuge functions. Mangrove fisheries play an important role in ensuring people's well-being, as they provide an accessible source of protein. The collection and processing of mangrove fish provides employment and income for many coastal communities.

When other sources of food provision fail, mangroves also have an emergency food provision function. Some species of mangrove-associated snails are readily harvested when there is no other food available to a household.

The steady supply of falling leaves from mangroves provide an abundant supply of food for microbes, which transform nutrients into a useful food source for larger consumers, including important fishery species. Its leaves

---

8   FAO – "Food and Agriculture Organisation of the United Nation Historical Role of Palms in Human Culture" in http://www.fao.org/docrep/X0451e/X0451e00.htm

are also ingested by crab and snail species; a number of which are directly consumed by people, and all of which provide an important source of food for larger crabs, prawns and fish, often of significant commercial value.

Many species of fish, including those of commercial importance, use the protection offered by mangroves as nursery sites when they are young and help to replenish offshore fish populations when they reach their adult size and swim out to sea. Some species show high dependence on mangrove nurseries, with adult populations significantly depleted in areas where nearby mangroves are lost.

In addition to benefiting fisheries operating directly within mangroves, the nutrients from the mangroves enhance the productivity of surrounding waters. These nutrient-rich waters create a feeding ground that attracts top predators such as groupers and snappers. The storm buffering capacities of mangroves, for example, can safeguard fishing grounds and protect fishing harbours from the ravages of extreme weather events.

Mangroves may also be interlinked with spiritual beliefs and practices such as festivals, religious rites, taboos and the establishment of sacred areas. For example, the Ikwerre have numerous myths of origin. There is a strong belief that *Chiokike* (Supreme Being) is the creator of the universe and its contents. *Chiokike* works in harmony with his other numerous subordinate beings or divinities, such as *Ali*, the earth divinity and the paramount divinity in the Ikwerre pantheon. The gods in the traditional religions were associated with the immediate environment.

The recreational, spiritual and cultural values of mangroves are difficult to capture but are nevertheless important for human well-being. Mangroves, sometimes in connection with adjacent terrestrial forests, sea grass beds and coral reefs, provide a variety of aesthetic and recreational experiences and cultural and artistic inspiration. Mangroves can be closely associated with deeply held historical, communal, ethical, religious and spiritual values. In some coastal communities, mangroves have been central to people's livelihoods for centuries and form an integral part of their cultural heritage and identity.

Mangroves of the Niger Delta are open to residents and tourists alike for recreational fishing, bird watching and wildlife. Mangroves may also provide opportunities for leisure, recreation and education. For instance, the traditional wrestling in Ikwerre that used to be an important sporting event is rooted in mythologies that associate leisure with the forest. In the Ikwerre mythology, once upon a time there was an encounter between a hunter and a gorilla that resulted into a wrestling contest. The gorilla taught wrestling techniques to our Ikwerre ancestors.

Nature works as a whole cycle. This is seen not only in animals where predator and prey work together but also in the different energy and nutrient cycles. Removal of trees results in lost habitat, putting thousands of species at risk of extinction. Deforestation of the Niger Delta region for the exploration and exploitation of petroleum products means taking a forest and destroying it. All the trees, plants, insects, animals and people who live there are either killed or forced to find a new home. Once a forest is cut down, the plant species all are gone. Insects and animals might make it out to find new homes, but that might include areas populated by humans, making their survival questionable. The indigenous people who live in their ancestral homes have to relocate to other areas altogether. This is a complete life change. The way they provide for their families and the very basic way they live their lives would be completely different.

As areas of tropical forests are destroyed or degraded, many communities in the Niger Delta are forced to change their resource base. In some cases, they move into areas occupied by other groups, thereby straining the area's resources. In other cases, they are forced to relocate outside of their ancestral homes, permanently altering their ways of life. Rarely are the rights of these groups to the lands they occupy recognised. Their intimate knowledge of the area's resources and how to manage them are nearly always ignored.

The Niger Delta and British Contact

The Niger Delta people have their lands near the delta of the River Niger in the southern part of Nigeria. This has historically been a fertile area especially for agricultural purposes before the emergence of hydrocarbon businesses in 1958. The Niger Delta has equally been a strategic trading outpost connected to global mercantilist capitalism even before the 17th century era of the obnoxious Trans-Atlantic Slave Trade. Beginning with the arrival of the Portuguese in the region in the 1480s, Niger Delta emerged as one of the most substantive points of commercial and political contacts between Africans and Europeans on the West African continent.

The bulk of what is now Nigeria became British Territory between 1885 and 1914, although some autonomous communities were not conquered and incorporated in the protectorate until the early twenties. Between the 15th and 19th centuries, European relationship with West African States were trade/commercial, with little or no political undertones. The Europeans depended on the coastal rulers not only for securing trade, but also for the safety of their lives and property. Thus, European traders went out of their way to ensure they were in the good books of native rulers. Professor Itse Sagay, a distinguished lawyer, concisely articulates this period thus:

> It should be noted that the main commodity during this period were human beings. This was the era of slave trade. It was in a bid to protect the lives, properties and trade of British traders that the British Prime Minister, Palmerston appointed John Beecroft as British Consul in Nigeria in 1849. This was the beginning of piecemeal British colonisation of the independent nations of what later became Nigeria.[9]

For several centuries, European trading nations including Portugal, France, England, and Holland were actively engaged in contacts with the people of Niger Delta. Then the economic activities of the region entailed mainly export of salt and fish to the hinterland.

Slave trade in the Niger Delta

9   Itse Sagay, "Nigeria: Federalism, the Constitution and Resource Control" in http://www.waado.org/NigerDelta/Essays/ResourceControl/Sagay.html

In the 18th century, when the slave trade was at its peak, the region was one of West Africa's largest slaves exporting area. As a coastal region, Niger Delta became a major source of slaves in the late eighteenth and early nineteenth centuries. It was a 'slave coast'. Here ,wars were waged and the whole economies were skewed towards satisfying the demands for slaves.

After the abolition of the slave trade at the beginning of the nineteenth century, British attention on the Niger Delta coast was turned towards 'legitimate trade' supplying trade goods in return for raw materials or semi processed commodities: in particular palm oil, a major lubricant for the industrial revolution.

At about the year 1861, some British firms established trading ports around the Niger Delta and subsequently extended their operations from the middle of the Niger valley into what is now known as Northern Nigeria. The companies later merged and formed a company known as Royal Niger Company which was granted a charter by the British monarch not only to trade but also to administer the area from the middle of the Niger valley to present-day Northern Nigeria.

Between 1880 and 1885, British officials had practically signed treaties with almost all the coastal chiefs. At the same time, the United African Company which was an amalgamation of all major British firms trading along the Niger coast and delta, was also busy signing treaties with the chiefs along the banks of Rivers Niger and Benue. In 1884, at the request of Portugal, German Chancellor Otto von Bismark called together the then major Western powers of the world to negotiate questions and end confusion over the control of Africa. Bismark appreciated the opportunity to expand Germany's sphere of influence over Africa and desired to force Germany's rivals to struggle with one another for territory. At the time of the conference, 80% of Africa remained under traditional and local control. What ultimately resulted was a hodgepodge of geometric boundaries that divided Africa into fifty irregular countries.

After the conference of 1884, all the territories occupied by the United African Company and territories that had signed treaties with the consuls came under effective British control without any meaningful British administration being set up. The British sphere of interest in the Niger basin was internationally recognised in 1885, as the second British outpost in the Niger River region, after Lagos (1862). The administrative centre (1885-1894) was at Bonny; British consuls were stationed at Old Calabar. However, in 1889, the British government appointed Major Claude Mcdonald to investigate the problems of Niger Delta administration. His recommendation of a Crown Colony for the Oil Rivers was rejected. Instead, the British government decided to proclaim a protectorate over the territories and in 1891, the Oil Rivers Protectorate was established with Major Mcdonald as the Commissioner. Consuls and Vice-Consuls were appointed. They worked under the supervision of a Commissioner who lived at Calabar. For the maintenance of law and order, an Armed Constabulary was established and was commanded by British officers.

In 1891, the Oil Rivers Protectorate was formally proclaimed, named after palm oil, the major export product. In 1893, it was extended and re-named the Niger Coast Protectorate. In 1900, this enlarged protectorate was amalgamated with the southern part of the territory that had been administered by the Royal Niger Company to form the Colony and Protectorate of Southern Nigeria[10] (1900-1914).

The Niger Coast Protectorate, which succeeded the Oil Rivers Protectorate, was created in 1893 with its headquarters at Calabar and Sir Ralph Moore as its first Consul-General. The new protectorate covered a wider area and extended further inland. The Niger Coast Protectorate had the same responsibilities as the Oil Rivers Protectorate, that is the promotion of trade as well as the protection of British traders in the new territory.

On the revocation of the charter of the Royal Niger Company on 31 December 1899, the area under its sphere of administration was renamed Protectorate of Northern Nigeria, with effect from 1st January 1900. The remaining part of the present-day Nigeria that did not form part of the Protectorate of Northern Nigeria was added to the Niger Coast Protectorate, which had earlier been established for the communities of the Niger Delta, to form the Protectorate of Southern Nigeria. That was the British colonial rule that provided the central authority that bound together all the erstwhile separate states, empires and kingdoms that were dotted all over the land mass now known as Nigeria. With the fiat of Lord Lugard in January 1, 1914, Nigeria became one political entity with the amalgamation of the Northern and Southern Protectorates. The amalgamation or seeming unification of these protectorates never put into consideration the socio-economic and political interests and aspirations of the numerous distinct ethnic groups. The assumption that every ethnic group in the arrangement would have access to the wealth and political power unhindered was a mirage from the onset.

---

10   Mobolaji E. Aluk, "Nigeria - from 1000 to 1999" in http://www.outcrybookreview.com/HistoryNigeria.htm

The amalgamation has two flaws. The first was the division of the country into three unequal regions, with the geographical size of the Northern Region alone exceeding that of the two Southern Regions put together. The second flaw involves the political and demographic domination of the Northern, Western, and Eastern Regions by the majority ethnic nationalities and the attendant marginalisation of the minority ethnic nationalities that comprise approximately one-third of the population of each region.

The Niger Delta people form the largest group amongst the ethnic minorities spread over Southern Nigeria. As already observed, the political history reminds us that the Niger Delta, as a region, predates Nigeria's emergence as a British Colony by at least a decade. Britain's Niger Delta Protectorate and the Niger Delta Coast Protectorate were already well established by the middle 1880s and the late 1890s before further British interests led to the formation of Southern Nigeria in 1900. That was the position of the minorities of the Niger Delta before 1914.

Niger Delta is rich in natural resources. It is home to crude oil. Before the discovery of crude oil in 1956, Niger Delta produced other cash crops such as cocoa, citrus, palm oil, cotton, yams, and cassava but the production of these crops ebbed with the discovery of crude oil. In Oloibiri, farmers migrated from rural to urban areas abandoning their crops—and their fertile lands—in quest of more lucrative businesses generated by oil wealth. Cocoa production, for example, declined sharply and the Nigerian Cocoa Board was abolished as the country failed to attend to aging cocoa plantations. At the same time, food import increased significantly while an increasing number of people drifted to the oil sector. Nigeria therefore transitioned from a multicultural to a monocultural economy to the detriment of the poor and the middle class. Yet, nowhere in the country were the consequences of such a transition felt more than the Niger Delta, the region that produces oil, which is the mainstay of the national economy.

Even though agriculture was a significant contributor to the Nigeria's GDP in the 1960s, total and per capita food production declined in the 1970s as oil displaced agriculture. Available data indicate that total export in oil increased over time from the late 20th century till it became the mainstay of Nigeria's economy.

NIGERIA EXPORTS

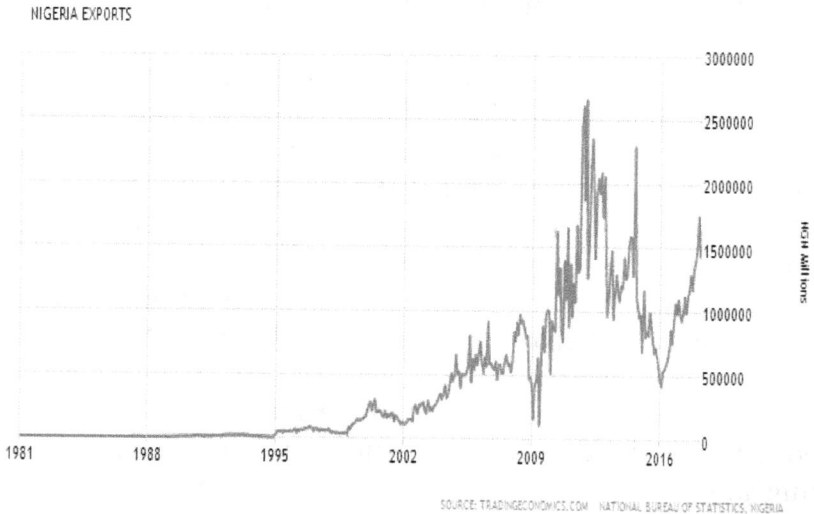

Nigeria total oil export

26

4

CRUDE OIL

Crude oil has been used in one form or another over thousands of years but it has become really important to the world economy in the last two centuries. Oil has become the most important source of energy since the end of World War II in 1945.

The first oil well was created in the middle of the 19th century in Pennsylvania, United States of America.[11] Edwin L. Drake in 1859 sank his first well in Titusville, Pennsylvania. He was a career railroad conductor who devised a way to drill a practical oil well. Before Drake, people around the world had gathered oil for centuries around "seeps," places where oil naturally rose to the surface and came out of the ground. By 1870, oil production had spread to other American states. During the latter part of the 19th century, oil was also produced in Canada and in European countries. The automobile boom of the early 20th century led to a higher demand of oil. It played an important role as the main fuel for tanks and planes in the two world wars. By 1950, the United States had become the world's largest oil producer. In the second part of the 20th century, Saudi Arabia and Russia produced even more than the USA.

Crude oil exists as a liquid that rests in various formations deep within the earth's crust. This liquid forms as a result of the decomposition of organic material that dates back

---

11   "Wikipedia, the free encyclopedia"

to millions of years. Another name used for this material is petroleum, though that term also refers to products made from the refined material itself. Petroleum literally means rock oil; oil that comes from rock. Petroleum is formed from organic matter (plants, animals and microbes) that is buried deep below the earth's surface by layer upon layer of sediment (sand, mud, etc.). Over long periods of time, the organic material is transformed by heat and pressure into crude oil.

Petroleum is lighter than water and so it moves upward through the ground water, which fills the tiny holes and crevices in the rocks, until it reaches an impermeable layer where the holes are too small for the droplets to pass through. There the oil remains until it is discovered by drilling a well.

Oil wells are drilled as deep as six miles[12] into the earth to search for petroleum. These wells can cost millions of dollars to drill, yet drilling is done because petroleum is a valuable natural resource.

Crude oil

---

12   Rosen, Jerome. "Deep Drilling: Probing Beneath the Earth's Surface." *Mechanical Engineering* (June 1991), 70-76.

Once extracted, crude oil undergoes distillation. This process breaks the liquid down into various products of different weights, depending on the exact composition of the liquid. There are thousands of products that we enjoy which come directly or indirectly from crude oil. Crude oil produces energy. Many petroleum products are energy carriers. When burned, the energy is released and can be harnessed for various products, like gasoline, diesel and jet fuel.

The Importance of Crude Oil

1. **Food:** Crude oil plays a part in the growth of our food. Fertilizer is something that relies on petroleum. When the price of oil goes up, it gets more expensive to grow food. Many of our food items are stored and or packaged in plastics also made from crude oil; meaning that crude oil plays a large part in the production of our food. This is one of the things that make high oil prices so scary. If it costs more money to grow, store, package, transport, and regulate the temperature of our food, then that cost will be passed on to the consumers!

2. **Plastic:** Crude oil is used in making plastic and this is probably the most widespread use of oil that many people associate with on daily basis. Plastic is used in just about everything that you can find in our homes. Plastic is used in the production of computer cases, shoes, cell phone, car bumpers, toys, and thousands of other everyday items. Some of our chairs, plates and cups are made of plastic.

3. **Clothing:** Petroleum is used to make clothing non-flammable and colourful. It is used in the production of rayon, nylon, polyester, and even artificial furs. Also, hangers are strengthened by petroleum-based resins.

4. **Furniture:** Our couch cushions are often filled with durable, lightweight polyurethane foam. Also, if you have carpet or linoleum flooring, you probably have a petroleum-based product in your home.

5. **Insulation:** The insulation that we have in our homes – which keeps unwanted heat from escaping or entering – is a petroleum-based product! This means that we depend on crude oil to regulate the temperature in our homes in more ways than we realise.

6. **Kitchen Items:** There are a number of items in our kitchens that rely on petroleum as part of their production. Our refrigerators, the molded interior panels, door liners, and even the foam insulation are all manufactured using crude oil. Many stoves function by using natural gas.

7. **Cars:** High-performance plastics have replaced heavier materials in vehicle making – from the interior to the engine block – reducing weight and improving fuel economy, and enhancing safety.

Crude Oil in Nigeria

The search for crude oil in Nigeria began as early as 1903 when the colonial government set up mineral survey corporation.[13] Unfortunately the search did not yield any significant result. In 1907, oil seep was observed at Araromi near Abeokuta. This observation led to a German company, Nigerian Bitumen Company to obtain license to explore oil deposits.

The Nigerian oil as an industry started in 1908 because the very first attempt to find oil in Nigeria was made in that year. Fifteen wells were drilled between 1908 and 1914

---

13 John M. Carland, *The Colonial Office and Nigeria, 1898-1914* (Basingstoke: Macmillan, 1985), 187.

without success. By 1937, the second attempt was made and this time by an Anglo-Dutch consortium called Shell D'Arey. Unfortunately, the outbreak of the Second World War interrupted the attempt. By 1947, Shell D'Arey came back as Shell BP Petroleum Development Company of Nigeria and drilled two exploratory wells between 1951 and 1955.

The first discovery of commercial quantities of oil in Nigeria was in 1956 at Oloibiri, about ninety kilometres west of Port Harcourt in what is now Bayelsa State. Other discoveries soon followed and exports began in 1958, although significant quantities only began to flow from 1965, with the completion of a terminal on Bonny Island, on the Atlantic coast, and pipelines to feed the terminal. In 1958, Nigeria was exporting about 17,000 barrels of oil per day (BOPD).[14]

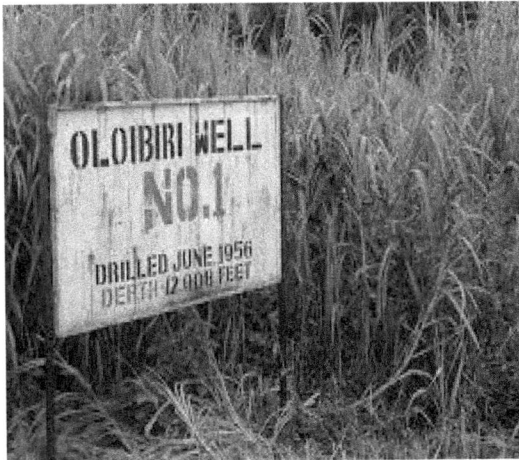

First oil well in Nigeria

---

14   "The Impact of Oil Sector on the Nigerian Economy" in http://www.datingswift.com/economics/the-impact-of-oil-sector-on-the-nigerian-economy

Between 1961 to 1962, the rights to explore oil were granted to other companies like Texaco Tenneco, Gulf (Chevron), Satrap (Elf) and Agip. Initially, all crude oil produced in Nigeria was exported without being processed. Most of the by-products of petroleum were imported because Nigeria had no refinery. By 1965, the first oil refinery was commissioned in Nigeria at Port-Harcourt.

At present, Nigeria has four refineries, with a combined installed refining capacity of 445,000 barrels per day (bpd). These four refineries are: the first Port Harcourt Refinery commissioned in 1965 with an installed capacity of 35,000 bpd and later expanded to 60,000 bpd; the Warri Refinery commissioned in 1978 with an installed refining capacity 100,000 bpd, and upgraded to 125,000 bpd in 1986; the Kaduna Refinery commissioned in 1980 with an installed refining capacity of 100,000 bpd, and upgraded to 110,000 bpd in 1986; the second Port Harcourt Refinery commissioned in 1989 with 150,000 bpd processing capacity, and designed to fulfil the dual role of supplying the domestic market and exporting its surplus.

The combined capacities of these refineries initially exceed the domestic consumption of refined products, chief of which is premium motor spirit (gasoline), whose demand was estimated at 33 million litres daily. The refineries have however been operating far below their installed capacities, as they are more or less abandoned due to administrative negligence, skipping the routine and mandatory turnaround maintenance that made products importation inevitable.

Estimates of Nigeria's oil reserves range from 16 billion to 22 billion barrels. Most of this oil is found in small fields in the coastal areas of the Niger Delta (According to the Ministry of Petroleum Resources, there are 159 oil fields, producing from 1,481 wells).

Nigeria's crude oil is probably the purest in the world. Generally called "sweet crude" as opposed to sour crude from Saudi Arabia and other regions, Nigeria Light has only 0.2% sulfur. From fractional distillation, you could get about 33% gasoline, 20% kerosene, 16% light gas oil, 30% heavy gas oils, leaving ONLY 1% bitumen residue. Compare these figures with, say, Boscan Venezuelan crude which has 6.4% sulfur, only 3% gasoline, 6% kerosene, 7% light gas oil, 26% heavy gas oils, and a whopping 58% bitumen residue.[15] This then is why Nigeria's crude is the dream oil of the advanced industrial countries of Europe and America: its lightness makes for cheaper distillation. These countries already have extensive road networks, so they have little or no interest in crude oil with high bitumen residue.

The price of Nigerian crude oil is linked to the price for Brent. Average operational costs in Nigeria are around U.S.$2.50 a barrel, higher than the Persian Gulf, but lower than the Gulf of Mexico and the North Sea.

The discovery of oil has transformed Nigeria's political economy, and oil has for the past two decades provided approximately 90 per cent of the country's foreign exchange earnings, and 80 per cent of federal revenue. Nigeria also has huge reserves of natural gas, yet to be fully explored. Yet, instead of turning Nigeria into one of the most prosperous states on the African continent, these natural resources have enriched a small minority while the vast majority have become increasingly impoverished. Nigeria is one of the poorest countries in the world. At the same time, the struggle among the elites to gain access to the profits of the oil has been a factor in the rule of successive governments.

---

15   "Coalition against Dictatorship (CAD), Nigerian Casefile: The Ken Saro-Wiwa-Ogoni Handbook; Compiled by the Coalition Against Dictatorship (CAD), 20 November 1995" in http://www.hartford-hwp.com/archives/34a/023.html

Politics has become an exercise in organised corruption; a corruption perhaps most spectacularly demonstrated around the oil industry itself, where large commissions and percentage cuts of contracts have enabled individuals to amass huge fortunes.

The following table is OPEC's oil production chart from 2016 - June 2018.[16]

Table 5 - 9: OPEC crude oil production based on *secondary sources*, tb/d

	2016	2017	4Q17	1Q18	2Q18	Apr 18	May 18	Jun 18	Jun/May
Algeria	1,090	1,043	1,014	1,014	1,022	990	1,035	1,039	4.6
Angola	1,725	1,637	1,628	1,562	1,487	1,511	1,519	1,431	-88.3
Congo	221	256	298	307	326	329	319	331	12.0
Ecuador	545	530	525	515	519	517	520	519	-0.9
Equatorial Guinea	160	133	129	134	127	127	127	126	-0.8
Gabon	221	200	199	195	187	185	187	190	3.5
Iran, I.R.	3,515	3,811	3,822	3,813	3,815	3,823	3,822	3,799	-22.7
Iraq	4,392	4,446	4,401	4,441	4,476	4,436	4,461	4,533	71.5
Kuwait	2,853	2,708	2,704	2,704	2,713	2,707	2,703	2,731	27.3
Libya	390	817	967	991	885	981	962	708	-254.3
Nigeria	1,556	1,658	1,760	1,780	1,685	1,764	1,632	1,660	27.8
Qatar	656	607	604	593	598	589	602	603	0.8
Saudi Arabia	10,406	9,954	9,975	9,949	10,110	9,898	10,015	10,420	405.4
UAE	2,979	2,915	2,892	2,850	2,875	2,868	2,862	2,897	35.1
Venezuela	2,154	1,911	1,762	1,538	1,387	1,433	1,388	1,340	-47.5
Total OPEC	32,864	32,628	32,681	32,385	32,212	32,156	32,154	32,327	173.4

16   http:// peakoilbarrel.com/opec-crude-oil-production-charts/

5

RESOURCE CONTROL
IN NIGERIAN FEDERALISM

In *The Wealth of Nations*, Adam Smith one of the pioneer economists pointed out that the principal factors of production are land, labour, capital and entrepreneurship.[17] Just as the price of labour is wages, capital has interest, entrepreneurship is driven by profit while rent and royalties are rewards for land ownership. Rent is a return for the use of the original and indestructible properties of the soil. Whoever owns a piece of land expects some form of compensation from those hiring this very important factor of production. The clamour for resource control is about controlling the land by those who own it. Government should then impose tax to be used for the welfare of the larger community.

In 2001, Senator David Dafinone[18] acknowledged that the statutory distribution of revenue from the Federation Account had been controversial as well as contentious. The Political Bureau Report of 1987 observed that the issue was so contentious that "none of the formula evolved at various times by a commission or by decree under different regimes since 1964 has gained general acceptability among the component units of the country."

---

17   Smith, Adam. *Wealth of Nations*, C. J. Bullock ed., Vol X *The Harvard Classics*. (New York.: P.F. Collier & Son, 1909–14), Bartleby.com, 2001. www.bartleby.com/10/.
18   "Resource Control: The Economic & Political Dimension by Senator David Dafinone" in http://www.waado.org/nigerdelta/essays/resourcecontrol/Dafinone.html

Nigeria is a federation. In a federal system of government, the power of the state is formally (constitutionally) divided among different levels of government. Each level of government is legally supreme over its own sphere. This is the opposite of the unitary system of government.

The term "Federal" has Latin roots; *Foederatus*. *Foederatus* is itself derived from the words *foedus* meaning contract, pact, treaty or convention; it implies an agreement.[19] In a federation, the federating units are not independent states. Instead, they are semi-autonomous (partially self-governing). The states within a federation possess autonomy, not sovereignty. However, the degree of autonomy, or self-government, is *substantial*.

The basic features of federalism include:[20]

- The decentralisation of authority from the centre to the states;
- A constitution that defines the powers and relationships existing between the centre and the states;
- A court of competent jurisdiction to interpret the relevant sections of the constitution in case of conflict between and among the tiers of government.

In a federal system, the national constitution protects the *right of each level of government to exist*. The national constitution recognises the existence of at least two levels of government in the country:

i.   The national, or central, government and

ii. The governments of the smaller regional communities or states.

The **national constitution** grants **substantial authority** to each of the two levels of government. Each level of government

---

19   Musa Adede, *Guided By Patriotism*, (Enugu, Snaap Press, 2013),
20   *Ibid.*

is given the right to make final decisions on at least some governmental activities and services.

In a federation, the national constitution gives the central government control over matters of *general,* or *common* concern to the country as a whole and gives the states the power to regulate matters of more local concern. Neither level of government in a federation receives its powers from the other. The states do not receive their powers from statutes enacted by the national legislature, and the national government does not receive its powers from decisions and actions of the state legislatures. Both levels of government. *"national and regional,"* receive their respective sets of powers from a common source, and that common source is the national constitution. The constitution of a federal system of government is not a product of the national literature alone, and that is why the consent of at least two third of the state houses of assembly is required to alter the constitution.

Federalism is usually practised in countries with many ethnic nationalities or groups with different backgrounds and peculiarities, with each group wanting its distinguishing identity to be maintained within the federation. That is why we have:

- United States of America with designated fifty "states."
- Australia with the six constituent political units of the federation called the "Commonwealth of Australia."
- Canada with the ten regional political communities designated as "provinces."
- Switzerland's 26 cantons are the federal states of the Swiss confederation.

Fiscal federalism encompasses principles of fiscal relations between federal and state governments, such as the command over resources by various levels of government and the direction and size of intergovernmental fiscal flows. This includes the division of tax power and the means through which resources are adjusted to match expenditure responsibilities for the federal and state governments. The major issues of fiscal federalism include:

- Constitutional allocation of expenditure responsibilities, which deals with the issue of which item of power of spending should be carried by which level of government;
- Constitutional allocation of revenue raising power; which deals with the issue of which types of taxes should be levied and non-tax revenues should be assumed in which jurisdiction by which level of government;
- Addressing the fiscal imbalance between the levels of government and disparities between them in executing their respective responsibilities;
- Addressing the intergovernmental financial transfer; which deals with the issue of financial flows between the federal and the states and among the states.

Presently, the Revenue Mobilisation Allocation and Fiscal Commission is in charge of revenue allocation as one of the constitutional functions of the commission. Part I, Paragraph 32 of the Third Schedule of the 1999 Constitution of the Federal Republic of Nigeria, states that the commission is to

> review, from time to time, the revenue allocation formulae and principles in operation to ensure conformity with changing realities. Provided that any revenue formula which has been accepted by an Act of the National Assembly shall remain in force for a period of not less than five years for the commencement of the Act.

At the moment, the factors in use are equality, population, landmass and terrain, internally generated revenue and social development factor. But the revenue allocation in Nigeria has a complicated history.

Revenue sharing and allocation between the federal and other tiers of government have become the most contentious issues in Nigeria's fiscal federalism. Revenue allocation has been a major issue in the Nigerian political system from the pre-independence era. Between 1946 and 1960, four fiscal review commissions were appointed to recommend a satisfactory revenue allocation formula for the country. The summary of the reports of the various commissions set up to look into revenue sharing is as follows:

SN	Year	Commission or Commission	Recommended Criteria	Other Basic Features of Recommendations
1	1946	Phillipson	(i) derivation (ii) even progress	Balance after meeting central government's budgetary need allocated to regions.
2	1951	Hicks-Philipson	(i) derivation (ii) fiscal autonomy (iii) needs, and (iv) national interest	Proportion of specified duties and taxes allocated to regions on the basis of derivation, special grant capitalisation, education and police.
3	1951	Chick	(i) derivation (ii) fiscal autonomy	Bulk of revenues from import duties and excise to the regions on the basis of consumption and derivation.
4	1958	Raisman,	(i) derivation (ii) fiscal autonomy. (iii) balance development (iv) need	Proportion of specified revenues distributed on the basis of derivation. Creation of distributable pool account (DPA) with

				fixed regional proportional shares: North 40%, West 31%, East 24%, and Southern Cameroon 5%.
5	1964	Binns	(i) derivation (ii) fiscal autonomy (iii) balance development (iv) need	Composition of DPA relative share slightly 30%, West 20% and Mid-West 8%.
6	1968	Diana	(i) even development (ii) derivation (iii) need (iv) minimum responsibility of government	Special grant account introduced, recommended the establishment of planning and fiscal commission. Recommendation rejected.
7	1970	Decree No. 13 of 1970	(i) population 50% (ii) equality of states 50%	Export duties of states reduced from 100% to 60%.
8	1971	Decree No. 9 of 1971	(i) population 50% (ii) equality of states 50%	Transferred rents and royalties of offshore petroleum mines from the states to the federal government.
9	1975	Decree No. 6 of 1975	(i) population 50% (ii) equality of states 50%	Onshore mining rents and royalties to states reduced from 45% to 20% Remaining 80% to the DPA. Import duties on motor spirit and tobacco to be paid 100% into the DPA. 50 of excise duties to be retained by the federal government, 100% to DPA.
10	1976	Decree No. 15 of 1976	(i) population 50% (ii) equality of states 50%	Regional proportion share of DPA split among the 12 new states,

				6 Northern states receive 7% each, East and Western states share in accordance with relative population.
11	1977	Aboyade	(i) equality of access 25%. (ii) national minimum standard 22% (iii) absorption capacity 20% (iv) independent revenue 18% (v) fiscal efficiency 15%	Replaced DPA with federation account. Fixed proportional share of this account between the federal 57%, states 30%, local government joint account created.
12	1981	1981 Act		Federation account to be shared: federal government 55%, state government 30.5%, local government 10%, special fund 4.5%.
13	1989	Decree No. 49 of 1989		Federation account to be shared: federal government 55%, state government 32.5%, local government 10%, special fund 2.5%.
14	1989	Danjuma		Equality of states 40%, Population 30%, social development effort 10%, Tax effort 10%, land mass 10%.
15	1989	Decree No. 49 of 1989	(i) equality of states 40%. (ii) population 30% (iii) internal revenue effort (iv) land mass (v) social development factor 10%	Federation account to be shared: federal government 47%, State government 10%, Local government 15%, special fund 8%.

16	1992	Decree No. 3 of January 1992		Federation account to be shared: federal government 50%, state government 25%, local government 20%, special fund 7%.
17	2009			Federation account to be shared: federal government 48.5%, state government 24%, local government 20%, special fund 7%.

6

WHEN OIL IS HELL

There is a saying: "Oil and water do not mix," but when oil spills on water, toxic chemicals from the oil do mix with the water and stay there for a long time. The thicker part of the oil spreads over the surface and prevents air from getting into the water, hence, fish, animals, and plants that live in the water are not able to breathe. When oil spills on water, the chemicals left behind may make the water unsafe to drink, even after the oil visible on the water is removed.

The word pollution has various meanings. Under the Nigerian law, Section 41 of the Federal Environmental Protection Agency Act defines 'pollution' to mean: "Man-made or man-aided alterations of chemical, physical or biological quality of the environment to the extent that is detrimental to that environment or beyond acceptable limits." In the specific case of oil pollution, it could be said that oil pollution occurs when the above happens as a result of, or in the course of the extraction, storage or transportation of petroleum oil.

When oil spills on land, it destroys the soil by choking out the air and killing the living things that make soil healthy. Something similar happens when oil gets on our skin or the skin of animals. The oil covers the skin and blocks air from getting in. Toxins from the oil also enter the body through the skin, causing illness. Although much of the world depends on the production or the trade of oil to fuel its economies, these activities can cause severe damage to the environment, either knowingly or unintentionally. Oil production, and/or transportation, can disrupt the human population, and the animal and fish life of the region. Oil waste dumping, production pollution, and spills wreak havoc on the surrounding wildlife and habitat. It threatens the survival of several plants, and has already harmed many land, air, sea animal and plant species in the Niger Delta.

Environmental Hazards of Oil Spillage

The effects of oil on marine life in the Niger Delta are caused by either the physical nature of the oil (physical contamination and smothering) or by its chemical components (toxic effects and accumulation leading to tainting). Marine life may also be affected by clean-up operations or indirectly through physical damage to the habitats in which plants and animals live. The animals and plants most at risk are those that come into contact with a contaminated sea surface: marine animals and reptiles; birds that feed by diving or form flocks on the sea; marine life on shorelines.

Runoffs from petroleum processing and petrochemical plants have dumped tons of toxic wastes into nearby waters. Gas and oil pipelines have stanched many creeks and rivers, swamping prime pastures and cropland. Furthermore, entire bays and lagoons along coasts have been fouled by oil spills and runoff of toxic chemicals.

The environmental damage that is a result of oil retraction and production have also directly affected human life in the region. Damages include pollution of water resources and contamination of the soil. Human beings are affected by environmental devastation because it is damaging to vegetation, livestock, and to the health of the human body itself.[21]

---

21 Acher AJ, Boderie P, Yaron B. (1989). "Soil pollution by petroleum products: 1. Multiphase migration of kerosene components in soil columns," *Journal of Contaminated Hydrology* 4(4):333-345

Water pollution caused by oil spillage

Stages of Oil Production and their Environmental Effects

1. **Exploration:** The search for oil often involves a series of explosions set off to help oil companies know what is underground. This is called seismic testing. Seismic testing damages homes, wildlife, and the land. When companies start looking for oil, forests are cut down and homes are destroyed, roads are built, and streams and rivers are blocked up.

2. **Oil drilling:** Oil wells are drilled to bring oil out of the ground. Oil drilling can cause fires, explosions, and other accidents that endanger workers and the community. When oil spills, it pollutes groundwater and waterways, harms plants and animals, and damages resources for hunting, fishing, and farming.

3. **Separation:** Oil comes out of the ground mixed with gas, heavy metals, and toxic water. The oil must be separated from these other materials. The dumping of the toxic water is often the largest cause of pollution in the Niger Delta. Laws about drilling in most countries

45

require the toxic water to be put back into the ground rather than dumped on the surface. This practice is usually not followed in Niger Delta. Oil companies in the Niger Delta most often do nothing more than dig a hole and dump in crude oil, drilling wastes, toxic water, and other wastes. These ponds often leak into the groundwater or overflow, contaminating groundwater and land.

4. **Transport and storage:** Wherever there is oil, there are oil spills. Ships and trucks have accidents, and pipelines leak. It is the oil companies' responsibility to prevent spills and to clean them up when they happen. Oil and oil products get spilled literally every day in the Niger Delta. Oil, stubbornly seeping through rusty pipelines and old wells contaminates the soil, kills all plants that grow on it and destroys habitats for mammals and birds. A rough estimate had it that 110,000 tons spilled in 2009.

More often, oil is often spilled during transport through pipelines, trucks, ships and leakages from storage tanks. These spills have caused and still cause damages to the soil, groundwater, animals, and people. Oil companies in the Niger Delta do not inform the communities when a spill happens. Moreover they do not usually contain the spill and clean it up right away. The main problem is that most of the pipeline infrastructures are deteriorated. And with fines, inexpensive and oversight lax, oil companies find it more profitable to patch up holes and pour sand on spills (or do nothing at all) than invest in quality infrastructure and comprehensive cleanups.

This spillage is a violation of a multitude of national and international laws and regulations on environmental pollution and damage. As a result of the high frequency of oil spills in the Niger Delta, many local communities have been destroyed, drinking water has been contaminated, and the ecosystem and soil composition have been altered irreversibly.

5. **Gas flares:** When oil is found together with natural gas, oil companies may burn the gas to separate it from the oil. This is called gas flaring. Gas flares expose workers, communities, and wildlife to pollution that causes cancer, skin diseases, asthma, bronchitis, and other health problems. The flares pollute the clouds, causing a "black rain" that poisons water sources. Burning gas makes giant flares that light up the sky and make a loud, terrible noise. Gas flaring is dangerous, wasteful, and very polluting. Selling the gas is a better and more reasonable alternative to burning it off but this is more costly and difficult because gas must be stored under pressure, increasing the risk of fires and explosions. This explains the reason why companies in the Niger Delta flare off the gas even though it increases the harm to people and the environment. Gas may be flared occasionally as a safety measure to prevent explosions (called safety flares), or every day as part of oil operations (called routine flares). Each kind of flaring requires a different response.

Flaring can be stopped! However, the worst routine gas flaring in the world occurred for many years in the Niger Delta of Nigeria. Gas flaring by international oil companies in Nigeria has cost many lives, and the poisons released by Nigerian gas flares have contributed more to climate change and global warming than all other sources in sub-Saharan Africa combined.

Comrade Che Ibegwura,22 a man from Rivers State, Nigeria, said: "For years, we have lived with continuous flaring of gas. Our farmlands have been polluted. We labour hard to plant, but little comes out. Our roofs are corroded. Our air is polluted. Our children are sick. Even the rainwater we drink is contaminated with black soot from the gas flares. We cannot continue with this suffering."

In 2005, after many years of protest and struggle, routine gas flaring was outlawed in the Niger Delta. A judge ruled that all the oil companies in Nigeria must stop gas flaring right away because of the health problems it causes, and because it violates the human right to a healthy environment.

Health Hazards of Oil Spillage

In places where oil is discovered, the economy develops rapidly, but it is an economy of misery. Poorly built oil camps are carved out of the landscape and bring with them many social problems, such as forced displacement, alcoholism and sexually transmitted infections. Oil companies and governments regularly wash their hands off the communities most damaged by oil development. These communities are often left on their own to try to determine how much and what kinds of harm oil has caused, and to search for ways to restore their community's health.[23]

Health problems from oil may be difficult to prove because they take a long time to affect people. But most people who live and work near oil drilling sites and refineries are familiar with the pollution of air and water

---

22   http://en.hesperian.org/hhg/A_Community_Guide_to_Environmental_Health:Gas_Flares
23   Oil, Illness, and Human Rights in http://hesperian.org/wp-content/uploads/pdf/en_cgeh_2012/en_cgeh_2012_22.pdf

from oil. Drilling for oil, refining it, and burning oil as fuel all lead to many serious health problems, such as:[24]

- Blurred vision and other eye problems
- Headaches, hallucinations, euphoria (sudden feelings of happiness), tiredness, slurred speech, brain damage, coma
- Convulsions and unusual deaths
- Nose sores and nose bleeds
- Ear infections
- Asthma, bronchitis, pneumonia and other respiratory diseases
- Lung and throat infections and cancers
- Increased risk of tuberculosis
- Heart attacks
- Digestive problems, including vomiting, ulcers, and stomach cancer
- Damage to liver, kidneys, and bone marrow
- Menstrual problems, miscarriages, stillbirths, and birth defects
- Skin rashes, fungus, and cancers.

Some long-term health effects

Reproductive health problems:[25] Breathing fumes or swallowing food or liquids contaminated by oil and gas causes reproductive health problems such as irregular bleeding cycles, miscarriages, stillbirths and birth defects. These problems may have early warning signs such as abdominal pain or irregular bleeding.

Cancer: Regular contact with oil and gas might be a cause of certain kinds of cancers. Children living near oil

---

24   http://en.hesperian.org/hhg/A_Community_Guide_to_Environmental_Health:Oil_
      Causes_Serious_Health_Problems
25   *Ibid.*

refineries are much more likely to suffer from cancer of the blood (leukemia) than those who live farther away. People living in areas where oil is drilled are much more likely to develop cancers of the stomach, bladder, and lungs than people living in other places. Workers in oil refineries are at a high risk of developing cancer of the lip, stomach, liver, pancreas, connective tissue, prostate, eye, brain, and blood.

Air pollution: Although an environmental hazard, air pollution has long-term health effect on humans. Air is polluted when it becomes contaminated with poisonous gases and small dust particles. Most air pollution is caused by burning fossil fuels (oil, coal, diesel, gasoline) to run engines, factories, and power plants. Wind and rain can carry air pollution far from where the pollution was made. This causes health problems for people everywhere. Air pollution is usually worse in cities and industrial areas like Port Harcourt and Warri, low-lying areas or those circled by mountains, and places where air gets trapped and does not move well. Air pollution causes serious health problems, including many cancers and respiratory illnesses. Air pollution causes acid rain that damages the human lungs, forests, water sources, and buildings and is also one of the main causes of global warming.

People in oil-rich areas hope that oil will bring wealth but in most cases, the wealth goes to the oil companies while the people in the communities are left with poverty, pollution, sickness, and the violence that seems to spill over wherever oil is found. However, because the world economy depends on oil, the oil industry has the power to influence governments and international policies to their advantage.

7

OIL BUNKERING IN THE NIGER DELTA

It is important to state in clear terms that oil bunkering, by its very nature, is a dark, obscure business. It is a complex business and extremely difficult to know how it operates. The illegal siphoning of oil off from pipelines, termed "bunkering," is an enormous criminal enterprise that runs through multiple layers and units of operators.[26] There are suspicions that the lack of effort to combat bunkering suggests that some members of the security forces and some highly placed persons must be complicit. Thus, it is possible to identify the main players involved in the oil bunkering business at its various levels.

Let us examine three categories of bunkering.

Pilfering: By definition, pilfering means to steal a small amount of something. Pilfering in bunkering is conducted by local people, those who are financially powerless and have no sponsorship. The illegal refineries do not drill, but tap from the established oil companies at the point of transporting the crude from one point to another. Skilled operators, usually welders, can install taps both on dry land and underwater. They often work in small teams of 3 to 6 people and can set up a tapping point in just a few days. During the tapping process, the pressure on pipes must be reduced before a tap can be installed. Unfortunately, this pressure is reduced by the corrupt oil companies' staff from

---

26   "How crude oil is stolen, refined, sold in Niger Delta" in http://www.premiumtimesng.com/news/150075-crude-oil-stolen-refined-sold-niger-delta.html

their control room. The installation of taps is the beginning of the illegal refinery production chain.

Once the tap is installed, a small team of about five workers guard and operate the tap, using the oil pressure and a rubber hose to siphon crude oil from the tap into a boat – Cotonou Boat – built to receive oil. Tap operators are well protected, but the taps locations are dangerous for outsiders. The Cotonou Boats transport the stolen crude from the point of tapping, through the creeks, to illegal refineries scattered around the creeks of the Niger Delta. A bulk of the stolen crude is transported to oil tankers waiting off the coast for national and regional markets. Average camps employ between 12 to 20 workers. The bulk of petroleum products produced at illegal refineries in the Niger Delta is diesel; it is therefore not a thing of surprise that some of the diesel in circulation are illegally refined.

Pilfering and illegal refinery

Refining diesel illegally is a very dangerous operation. The smoke, heat and explosions from the process have killed very many young people because they cannot escape the flames. The aim is to boil barrels of oil to evaporate the diesel which then passes down a rusted pipe, cooled by water, and drips out slowly into a container at the other end. Heating oil to such temperatures with such basic equipment is dangerous. Having the distilled diesel only a few meters from a naked flame could be lethal. The surrounding trees and earth are blackened from the flames and explosions.

Large Scale: A second type of illegal bunkering involves stealing crude oil either by hacking into the pipeline directly or by tapping the wellhead. This process involves removing the structure at the top (called the Christmas tree) and attaching a hose to siphon off the oil. From there, the oil is placed on small barges and taken out to the sea, where it is loaded into large ships lurking out of sight of the authorities.

Wellhead

In return for their oil, the bunkers' receive money and weapons. The large tankers (which generally carry between 30,000 and 500,000 barrels of crude, but can carry up to two million barrels) usually take their cargo to spot markets. There are large international syndicates involved in this operation, which also handle the money laundering for the international players. While Niger Delta youth may handle the local tapping and loading, international players play roles in financing, transporting, and laundering the money associated with blood oil. Similarly, there is also the suspicion that top Nigerians are actively involved in the large-scale bunkering business.

Excess Lifting: The third type of illegal bunkering involves the excess lifting of crude oil beyond the licensed amount, using forged bills of lading, which are the documents issued by a carrier to a shipper, listing and acknowledging receipt of goods for transport and specifying terms of delivery. This type of bunkering often involves a number of oil companies' staff and Nigeria's state oil company, the Nigerian National Petroleum Corporation (NNPC), as well as top government officials who give the oil lifting contracts.

Attempts to Tackle Oil Bunkering in Nigeria

Several attempts have been made to control bunkering in the past in Nigeria. However, these efforts are usually not sustained or properly executed. Some of the attempts include:

Arresting bunkers' and traffickers: There have been several attempts to arrest those involved in the bunkering and trafficking of oil. However, these actions seldom lead to successful prosecutions. In spite of improved equipment for the Nigerian Navy, there are no marked improvements in the patrolling of coastal waters.

Closing markets for illegal oil: There have been efforts to close markets for illegal oil. In 2003, the government issued warning to some countries that were engaging in illegal trade and at the same time offered contracts for the supply of legal oil to the state-owned refineries of some West African countries. This method proved to be effective.

Increasing military presence in the Niger Delta: The introduction of the Joint Task Force (JTF) in the Niger Delta has not had the desired effect of controlling the illegal trade. On the contrary, it has alienated the people and provided opportunity for some to participate in the bunkering business and to extort money from local communities.

Introducing the Nigerian Extractive Industries Transparency Initiative: The Nigerian Extractive Industries Transparency Initiative (NEITI) is the Nigerian version of the Extractive Industries Transparency Initiative (EITI), an international strategy launched by a coalition of non-governmental organisations (NGOs) and supported by scores of governments and international oil companies. It aims to strengthen governance by improving transparency and accountability in the extractives sector. It sets a global standard for companies to publish what they pay to governments in taxes, commissions, and royalties and for governments to disclose the revenues that they receive.

Making public offers of military support and training: Some foreign governments publicly offered military support to Nigeria but it resulted in an uproar against "foreign military presence in the Niger Delta." Similar but less public offers by military training have been rejected, with the Nigerian government requesting military equipment instead.

Developing oil thumbprinting technology: Oil thumb printing is an analytical technique developed by chemists to identify the unique characteristics and composition of oil. Its proponents claim it is sensitive enough to identify oil emanating not only from Nigeria but also from particular fields or even specific wells.

Offering electronic bills of lading: Paper versions of bills of lading can be easily forged by either increasing or decreasing the stated volume of oil carried or changing its place of origin. As a cargo moves from place to place, the bills of lading can be altered to disguise illegal additions. However, electronic bills of lading are far better because they are virtually impossible to forge.

Supplying coastal surveillance equipment: This equipment was supplied and installed. The equipment uses radar sonar infrared to monitor ships on Nigerian waters, but till date, there appears to be little or no feedback on what has been observed. Some international bodies also proposed assistance in tracing small arms, stockpile management, and carrying out stop-and-search operations. However, these offers have not been accepted.

Discussing maritime safety and security: In the past, some international bodies were interested in discussing the issue of maritime security with the Nigerian military, but Nigerian officials were primarily interested in the provision of new equipment, such as boats and rocket launchers.

Involving the United Nations: The United Nations has repeatedly offered assistance to Nigeria in addressing the core problems of the Niger Delta. Four advisers were posted to the office of the Vice President in early 2008 but left in frustration six months later when they were unable to gain access to the people and information they needed to fulfill their stated duties.

Recommendations for Tackling Bunkering Oil

Putting an end to the trade in stolen oil can only be achieved through concerted, coordinated, and sustained action by Nigeria, the international community and technical support from multilateral organisations. The following are some of the steps that could be taken to tackle the scourge:

- The trade in stolen oil is a purely criminal enterprise, but the Nigerian government must recognise that its disastrous neglect of the Niger Delta has helped the act to flourish. The Nigerian government must work harder to address the socioeconomic grievances of the people of the Niger Delta. The Niger Delta region remains pitifully underdeveloped, and its people have had to contend with the destruction of their environment and their traditional means of livelihood.

- The government could go a long way toward building confidence and harnessing goodwill in the Niger Delta by improving the local infrastructure through a road-building project. This would not only have the benefit of improving the transport network in the region but it would also provide jobs for unemployed youth whose current options are limited to criminal enterprises such as oil bunkering.

- The report of the Niger Delta Technical Committee contains a number of important recommendations, notably an immediate increase in the percentage of oil revenue given back to states by the federal government from 13 per cent to 25 per cent. The committee calls for this percentage to further rise over time, reaching 50 per cent within several years. Increasing the amount of money oil-producing states receive for their own resource would be a powerful way of easing the sense of neglect felt by the people of the Niger Delta. Other recommendations include clamping down on the illegal supply of small arms and light weapons to the Niger Delta, which fuels the insurgency and gives those involved in oil bunkering formidable armouries with which to fight their opponents. Identifying the highly placed people inside and outside of government who are engaged in sponsoring violence for economic and political gain should equally be addressed.

- The government should show faith in the people of the Niger Delta by awarding oil contracts and blocs to competent local communities and handing out scholarships to those youths who show promise.
- Making high-profile arrests of some of the key players in the bunkering business and successfully prosecuting them would send out a powerful message that the government is serious about ending oil bunkering.
- The coastal surveillance system that was piloted in 2008 should be expanded and the information it gathers should be shared more effectively with relevant parties.
- Relatively cheap and unsophisticated surveillance equipment can be used to monitor attacks on oil pipelines and track the movements of suspicious cargo around the Gulf of Guinea. Remote sensors can be placed on pipelines, which are able to detect acts of vandalism.
- Nigeria can adopt the moral high ground by taking tough action domestically against oil bunkering, then encouraging other countries to do the same. She should make clear to her international partners that accepting stolen crude from Niger Delta is unacceptable and will not be tolerated.
- The Nigerian government is ill-equipped to deal with the problems posed by the trade in illegal oil. Civil society will therefore have to take a leading role in ensuring that the issues of the Niger Delta are kept on the political agenda. There have been several cases of people in the Niger Delta being killed for exposing individuals they suspected of being members of armed groups. Those who expose people involved in oil bunkering are likely to face similar risks.

- Although the Nigerian government has repeatedly requested assistance in addressing the problem of oil bunkering, it has not always accepted such assistance. The international community must take this request literally and hold Nigeria to its stated commitment.

- Nigeria's international partners can share information and help trace the money trail from oil bunkering. Interpol or NGOs, such as Global Witness, can trace and expose these money trails. If possible, this money should be frozen and repatriated to the Nigerian government.

- The Nigerian government should expand dialogue to include more international players. The more unified the international approach, the more effective it will be.

- A solid security sector reform process should be undertaken to restore the competence of the Nigerian military.

Other Recommendations by Various Reports

THEME	NAME OF REPORTS & PAGE IN THE REPORTS	RECOMMENDATIONS
Gas Flaring	Ogomudia report pg 31 pt 33 (2001)	All gas flaring should be terminated in 2008 with no further deadline or extension.
Gas Flaring	Vision 2010 pg 23 (1996)	Nigeria contributes substantially to the depletion of the ozone layer. Nigeria's contributes 28% of the total global flare.
East West Road	Belgore Report pg 18 pt 2, 3 (1992)	East- West Road which traverses the major oil producing states should be dualised and improved; East-West rail line should be constructed from Calabar to Lagos and to link the line to an improved national rail network.
Militancy	Coastal States Report pg 40 pt 7 Women's Conference pg 45 pt 3	Militants should be used for surveillance jobs for oil installation in the Niger Delta as has already been done under the GMOUS being signed with communities by some oil companies, particularly Shell and Chevron. The demilitarisation of the Niger Delta and the immediate withdrawal of all military personnel from the region.
Youth	Ogomudia Report pg 28, Pt 2 (2001)	Appraise the negative impact of youth and community agitations and recommend measures to reduce youth restiveness, communal agitations and other

		incidents of sabotage of pipelines in oil communities.
Youth	White paper Pg 32, Pt 3, (2003)	The existing National Youth Policy should be promptly and faithfully implemented by government so as to address all aspects of social and economic inadequacies that predispose youths to violence and manipulation.
Youth	Urhobo Summit Pg 43, pt ¾ (1998)	Immediate and unconditional implementation of the federal government policy which restricts employment of non-skilled labour entirely to indigenes of oil-producing areas and at least 70% of skilled labour to indigenes. Oil companies operating in the region to implement fully its June 1994 policy on indigenous contractors and employment.
Security	UNDP HDR 2006, Pg 88 pt 7	Pursuit of sustainable partnership for the advancement of human development.
Security	Kaiama Declaration pg 42 part 3 (1998)	The military should be redeployed away from their territories.

8

THE NIGER DELTA CONFLICT

No region of the Federal Republic of Nigeria has been more misunderstood, misheard, mistreated, misjudged, misrepresented and misreported outside itself than the Niger Delta. Regrettably, most people who speak about Niger Delta have never lived in and have no in-depth knowledge of this Sahara desert of poverty. Perhaps the most enduring, even if not the most accurate image of the Niger Delta region for some years now has been that of a region of violence perennially on the edge of survival. Niger Delta, thus, stands singled out as a region of uniquely violent politics, a region where force makes the everyday life of the people even more demeaning and demanding than in other poorer parts of the country.

The rising violence in the oil-rich Niger Delta has continued to take its toll on Nigeria's revenue as the report by the Niger Delta Technical Committee revealed that the country lost at least $24 billion to oil theft and sabotage in the first nine months of 2008.[27] This intransigence can be attributed to the fact that most people feel they receive little or no benefit from the presence of the oil exploring facilities. For the Nigerian government which loses millions of dollars a day during such conflicts and of course for the companies, such a volatile security situation must be addressed as a priority. The conflict is not conducive to

---

27   *This Day Newspaper,* 9th April 2009, Nigeria: Niger Delta - Country Loses U.S. $24 Billion Oil Revenue in Nine Months.

the smooth-running of international business interests and as such is of grave concern to the domestic political and business elites.

There are currently two profoundly disturbing facts in support of economic and political antecedents to the Niger Delta conflict. The first is that, the income of the average person living in the Niger Delta has fallen by one per cent a year, every year since 1980, that is for about three decades. The second is that, some of the Niger Delta communities occupy the bottom positions among the list of undeveloped communities in Nigeria. So far, some of the communities in the Niger Delta region are not only poor but are getting poorer.

What about our natural resources? Since 1960 the use of lumber has multiplied while the forest is diminishing, the demand for fish has increased while the waters are polluted, grain consumption has multiplied, fuel burning has increased, and air and water are pollutants multiplied several folds. The unfortunate reality is that the economy continues to expand, but the ecosystem on which it depends does not, creating an increasingly stressed relationship. While economic indicators such as investment, production, and trade are consistently positive, the key environmental indicators are increasingly negative. Forests are shrinking, water tables are falling, soils are eroding, wetlands are disappearing, fisheries are collapsing, range lands are deteriorating, rivers are polluted, temperatures are rising, and plant and animal species are disappearing. All these, coupled with greed and perceived injustice are the causes of conflict around the world of which Niger Delta clashes are only patterns.

In Search of the Causes of the Niger Delta Conflict

There have been several stages in the debate about what are the root causes of the conflict in the Niger Delta. The causes of armed conflict in the Niger Delta are numerous and interconnected, ranging from individual or group volition to structural inequality and injustice. Some causes of conflict are local; others are the result of transformations in the international structure. Although the quality of governance in a few states and local governments have improved in the last decade, the structures of village and clan solidarity are steadily eroding. Continuing economic decline and material insecurity are accompanied, in many villages in the region, by increasing political instability.

One problem in the academic literature[28] is that it usually focuses attention on the question: which is the most important cause of armed conflict. In most cases, however, this is a misleading way to look at the issue of the Niger Delta. The question is not which cause is more important than any other, but rather how do the different causes interact? In particular, the attempt to force a choice between economic and political explanations of armed conflict is misguided. Violent conflict can easily develop if a large number of people become convinced that taking up arms is not only legitimate but perhaps the only way to secure the necessities of life. In other words, they feel that they are in an unjust situation and must therefore decide to rectify it.

However, a large number of people does not make such decisions spontaneously. The series of conflicts in the Niger Delta over the last two decades have produced complex emergencies that have led to various combinations of famine, destruction of infrastructure, enforced displacement of populations and regional destabilisation. There are now

---

28   Collier Paul, and Anke Hoeffler, "Resource Rents, Governance, and Conflict" in *Journal of Conflict Resolution 49, no. 4* (2005): 625–633.

violent situations in almost every state of the Niger Delta region which produce hundreds of victims per year in the violent struggle over political power or territory. These conflicts are part of, and instrumental to, illegal economies based mainly on crude oil and on illicit trades of weapons.

For about two decades now, the Niger Delta is the scene of Nigeria's worst internal conflict and poses the biggest challenge to the territorial integrity of the nation. In the Niger Delta, a system of profit, power and protection that benefits certain groups has emerged. It has been observed that some Niger Delta political elites and conflict entrepreneurs are beneficiaries from the continuation of the conflict, even as other sections of the community become increasingly impoverished. To a certain extent, this largely explains the continuation and the complexity of the violent conflict.

Demand for Resource Control

The primary cause of conflict in the Niger Delta is competition over declining resources. The central role of the state in determining resource distribution makes it a major target and, when power is over-centralised, there is bound to be conflict. Resource scarcity and competition in the Niger Delta arise from the natural resource base, population pressures, and environmental degradation. The natural resource base, topography, and climate are contributing factors to conflict. The history of the region includes massive population movements pushed by other groups and pulled by the search for better farming and fishing opportunities.

The Problem of Greed

The decision to take up arms is a complex process involving many actors in a wide range of conditions and circumstances. Conflict would not occur or persist if it did not have significant political and economic functions and benefits for political power groups. These groups can be divided into those who actively manipulate violence due to greed and those who are ready to be manipulated into violent activities due to their need. Since they can profit, authorities often calculate they have much more to gain from continued war than from peace

Presently, there is the thrust of the argument that greed is in fact, the silent force of the conflict in Niger Delta. The most common answer in the fast-growing literature on civil wars is that lootable[29] wealth, defined as lucrative, easy-to-transport resources such as crude oil, generates disorder by supplying the motive and means for conflicts. Pointing to a strong and positive statistical association between lootable resources and political disorder, scholars argue that lootable wealth is a "honey pot" that fuels "greed-based" insurgencies.

Grievances

Another possible mechanism which has been widely cited by policy analysts and journalists is a "grievance" mechanism.[30] It suggests that resources extraction creates grievances among the local population, due to land expropriation, environmental hazards, insufficient job opportunities and the social disruption caused by labour migration. These grievances, in turn, lead to conflict. The problem in the Niger Delta is also the culmination of government insensitivity to the grievances of the local people and the oil companies

---

29   Collier Paul, "Economic Causes of Civil Conflict and Their Implications for Policy" in *Leasing the Dogs of War*, eds. Chester A. Crocker, Fen Osler Hampson et al, (Washington.: DC, United States Institute of Peace, 2007),

30   *Ibid.*

policies that failed to address environmental degradation. One of the fundamental grievances of Niger Delta people concerning environmental abuse is the complete lack of concern for ecological rehabilitation, even in view of expert judgment that oil and gas are exhaustible resources.

> The grievances of the local people are based on environmental damage of the region by oil exploration and exploitation, their rights to fair share of the oil revenue, and their collective oppression as a minority by Nigeria's ethnic majorities. This accounted for an attempt by a small group of Ijaw activists (the Niger Delta Volunteer Force) led by Isaac Adaka Boro, Sam Owonaro and Nottingham Dick, to secede from Nigeria through force of arms by proclaiming the Niger Delta Republic in February, 1966.[31]

The grievances of the Niger Deltans have involved three closely interrelated, but analytically distinct issues: firstly, that all laws relating to oil exploration and land ownership be abrogated; secondly, the issue of natural resource control and self-determination; and thirdly, that appropriate institutional and financial arrangements should be put in place by the Nigerian nation state and the oil multinationals should compensate the oil-producing communities for the developmental and environmental problems associated with oil exploration and exploitation. The conflict has therefore been made complex and worse by the goal-blocking attitude exhibited by the parties.

Resources extraction creates grievances among the local population, and those grievances, in turn lead to conflicts. Klare for example,[32] suggests that "resource wars" are caused in part by logging or mining firms that are "ravaging the environment" and "driving off the people who have long inhabited the area."[33]

31   J ELEAZU, Nigeria: *The First 40 Years*, (Ibadan, Standard, 2006), 212.
32   KLARE M, *Resource Wars: The New Landscape of Global Conflict*, (New York, Metropolitan Books , 2001), 208.
33   *Ibid.*

Poverty

Endemic poverty and wide inequalities of income are reliable predictors of conflict. Poverty limits opportunities to education, employment and economic advancement. This lack of opportunity can intensify the sense of grievance among social groups suffering discrimination. When opportunities are scarce, discrimination can take away any hope of finding employment. In tearing the last shreds of hope, it causes deep resentment and destroys any sense among its victims that they have a stake in society. The denial of opportunity and impoverishment of people linked by primordial ties undoubtedly contributed to the strength of societal resistance to the state.

The majority of the Niger Delta people live in poverty

Poverty in the Niger Delta is a rural phenomenon. The top 5 per cent of the population enjoy over 80 per cent of the income that comes to the region. As the majority of people in rural areas depend on agriculture as their primary occupation, the unequal distribution of agricultural land has consequences in poverty. Land distribution and gross disparities in land ownership are some of the major causes of poverty, injustice and social discrimination. Due to such disparity, a large number of people have no access to productive land resources.

The insurgency is more violent in villages historically characterised by rural poverty, low literacy rate, dominated by ethnic people, frequent victims of starvation, and higher percentage of the unemployed. National and international developmental organisations are working hard to change the conditions of those areas. However, they have failed to strengthen the capacity and commitment of state structures or to change practices at local level to any marked degree. In some cases, their role is counterproductive. After the return of democracy in 1999, the problems faced in rural areas remained unaddressed: locals were excluded from development processes and the gap between the more urban and the rural population was broaden. Unemployment and underemployment, especially among the youth, have created a space for the militia to operate. The attraction of mainly poor and illiterate villagers to join the militia cannot be linked back to resistance political theory, but rather to the promises of a better future. This means, incidence of insurgency is high in those areas that are rated low economically.

The presence of a high proportion of young men in a society also increases the risk of conflict, whereas the greater the educational endowment, the lower the risk. Education is relatively more important than the proportion of young men available. Thus, some societies are much more prone to conflict than others, simply because they offer more inviting economic prospects for rebellion. A country with large natural resources, many young men and little education is very much more at risk of conflict than one with opposite characteristics.

The armed conflict in the Niger Delta is a multi-faceted problem. Not only does it produce human tragedies on a large scale, it also creates humanitarian crises, contributes to global and regional insecurity, and perpetuates poverty. For all of these reasons, ending conflict or reducing its intensity must be a very high policy, imperative in the development agenda.

Major Actors in the Conflict

It is hard to say who is to blame for the violence that has wrecked the Niger Delta region. Since the beginning of Shell's operations in the Niger Delta, the oil companies have wreaked havoc on neighbouring communities and their environment. Apart from physical destruction to plants around the flaring areas, thick soot are deposited on building roofs of neighbouring villages. Whenever it rains, the soot are washed off and the black ink-like water runs down the roofs and is believed to contain chemicals which adversely affect the fertility of the soil. Many of the operations and materials of the oil companies are outdated, in poor condition and would be illegal in other parts of the world. The high-pressure pipelines were constructed above ground through villages and crisscross over land that was once used for agricultural purposes, rendering it economically useless.

Some villagers and human rights groups also blame the oil companies and their contractors who hire young people and manipulate the Nigerian Armed Forces for their sole benefits. The presence of the multinational oil companies has done little to lift the local people out of poverty. This lack of socio-economic development is of apparent concern to local politicians who now recognise that the disproportionate scale of poverty in the Niger Delta can no longer be ignored. This is a real problem. Some of the people in the Niger Delta are disenchanted with the rhetoric of the government and are more inclined to supporting the rebel movement.

There are those who blame the federal, state and local governments who collect and distribute millions of dollars in the names of local residents who are yet to see any benefit for the sacrifices they make. In the Niger Delta, people feel aggrieved that the profits from their resources have been 'plundered' by the government. Throughout Nigeria, the population has experienced uneven development. Niger Delta communities have not enjoyed the same level of economic and social benefits as other areas of Nigeria like Abuja or Kaduna. When one considers that many of the Niger Delta communities have vast natural resources, it is not difficult to understand why many believe they are almost totally disengaged from the local economy. In the Niger Delta, there has been disenchantment with the federal government for many years. Federal officials acknowledge that corruption is a big problem but point out that even if Nigeria is having an oil boom, it does not amount to great wealth per capita.

9

POVERTY AS A TOOL FOR CONFLICT ENTREPRENEURS IN THE NIGER DELTA

Poverty situation in the Niger Delta today is frightening. Millions of people are homeless, disease is rampant, and starvation is a common occurrence. These are consequences of the devastation of the environment by the exploration and reckless exploitation of crude oil. As a result, people die from preventable diseases like malaria or diarrhoea. These also lead to lack of food which leads to malnutrition, vitamin deficiency, and ultimately, a painful death. Access to clean drinking water is also rare.

The future for most children in the Niger Delta looks bleak because without support, an early end to life is the only escape from reality as some of these children are orphaned at an early age, because of malnutrition and conflicts.

A comprehensive description of poverty in the Niger Delta will also include the following:

- Unequal distribution of income;
- High population growth;
- Illiteracy;
- Large families;
- Ethnicity;
- Problems of rural poverty;
- Malnutrition, diseases and long term health problems;

- Unhygienic living conditions, lack of proper housing; high infant mortality rate, injustice to women and ill-treatment of certain sections of the society.

The poor talk about various dimensions of poverty expresses people's frustration over their powerlessness and voicelessness. Being a complex concept, poverty is not easy to define as it can mean different things to different people. At least six interlocked dimensions feature prominently in poor people's definitions of poverty.

- *First:* Hunger and lack of food remain core concerns of the poor.

- *Second:* Poverty also has important psychological dimensions. In explaining poverty, the poor often express a sense of hopelessness, powerlessness, voicelessness, dependency, shame and humiliation.

- *Third:* Poor people often lack access to basic infrastructure such as roads, transport, clean water, electricity and marketplaces.

- *Fourth:* While literacy is clearly valued, schooling receives little mention or mixed reviews. This might be due to poor quality of education or lack of job opportunities for the educated people.

- *Fifth:* The poor dread serious illness within the family more than anything else since poor health can lead to job loss. Getting treatment can also entail large health care expenses, therefore, pushing the family into further poverty.

- *Sixth:* Lack of access to assets and basic needs such as education, health care and safe drinking water are some of the most critical issues concerning poverty and development. The poor mention income only infrequently. They focus on managing assets including human, social, physical and environmental assets as a way to cope with their vulnerability.

Over-Crowded Cities and Poverty

Fifty years ago, Africa was still considered a continent with the lowest degree of urbanisation because only three of African cities were listed by the United Nations among the world's 100 largest cities. But in recent decades, the Niger Delta is certainly among the most rapid population growth and urban change of any of the world's regions. Many factors wear away the economic stability of the city which in return multiply the pain of poverty, corruption, injustice, kidnapping and political/ethnic conflicts.

In most urban cities like Port Harcourt, Benin, Calabar and Warri, there is a general deterioration in public services, infrastructure and growing unemployment in the formal sector. More so, in place of the "self-help city" appears the "informal city" of the small-scale street vendor and hawker, the road-side food seller while poverty which is an old problem in Nigeria is being dramatised more in the cities of the Niger Delta.

Up to two-third of the Niger Delta population is under 25 age group while more than 45 per cent is under the age of fifteen. This disproportionate number has the tendency to grow considering the recent analysis of population growth rate. With poverty around them, young people roam the streets in the cities. They are found in the city's dumps scambling for recyclable items such as paper, plastic, glass, and scrap metals. They are without affection or education, security of family life. They are also abused and maltreated by adults whom they regard as enemies. Young children under the age of fifteen are abducted from the streets to become cult members. In some urban places, the exploitation of female children is on the increase. Masters rape servant girls while older men have unholy affairs with their relations. In the same vein, school girls are lured into prostitution in order to get pocket money.

In a region that has experienced different dimensions of conflict for more than 20 years, children have regularly been recruited. The recruitment and use of children in the Niger Delta should be viewed in the context of widespread poverty, lack of opportunity, lack of access to education and employment, and complete failure of the rule of law. But the government has limited reach in areas controlled by the militants.

Young People and Conflict: Poverty As a Catalyst

A key issue in the general problem of poverty is the lack of economic prospects for the young generation. Young people can negatively influence crises and violent conflicts. Because of lack of economic prospects and exclusion from the regular economy, they form a major pool of human resources for markets of violence and criminal structures. What is experienced now is that, many young people are being excluded from the regular economy, just as traditional structures are breaking down at the same time. The young generation is thus becoming an inexhaustible resource for criminal entrepreneurs such that where there are no prospects, the availability of instruments of violence begin to exert a powerful appeal. With a gun in hand, a young man can intimidate people and demand for false respect which could be shown to him by other people. Such false-respect could be the first time in his life, even though it is simply as a result of sheer terror on the part of the persons threatened.

In the Nigerian context, violence is also imposed from above by the privileged elites against the impoverished majority of the population. The concept of horizontal inequality assumes that collective violence is most likely to occur when groups experience a relative reduction in their opportunities or when there is a sudden worsening of their living conditions.

Crisis Prevention

The rural people of Niger Delta are poorer partly because they live in remote polluted areas, and are unhealthy and illiterate to have higher child/adult ratios, who work in insecure and low-productivity occupations. The rural poor have few human assets; with the head of the household likely to be an illiterate as a result of high dependency ratios, correlated with poverty, independently reduce the access to schooling. It is especially among the poor that girls have worse chances of education than boys.

Preventing such conflict situations could be done in three phrases[34] in which different efforts take place:

- *Early prevention* (primary prevention), which prevents the emergence of violent conflicts.
- *Late prevention* (secondary prevention), which prevents further escalation and spread of violent conflicts.
- *Continuous prevention* (tertiary prevention), which is intended to prevent the recurrence of violent conflicts.

Opinions are divided about the role of poverty or social alienation in the attraction to militancy. The poorest of the poor are not likely to have the means or energy to get

---

34   Boutros Boutros-Ghali, "Challenges of Preventive Diplomacy: The role of the United Nations and its Secretary-General" in Kevin M. Cahil ed, *Preventive Diplomacy, Stopping Wars before They Start,* (New York: Basic Books and the Center for International Health and Cooperation, 1996), 18.

involved in organised militancy since conflict entrepreneurs are rarely poor. However, poverty may inspire willing foot soldiers for conflict entrepreneurs, but conflict entrepreneurs generally have their own agenda which have little to do, except rhetorically, with the alleviation of poverty.

Militancy and Amnesty Programme

Governance and addressing conflict in the Niger Delta are serious issues. On 26 June 2009, the federal government announced the intention to grant amnesty and unconditional pardon to militants in the Niger Delta. A 60-day period was allowed for armed youths to surrender their weapons in return for training and rehabilitation by the government. The strategy of buying off militant leaders and clamping down militarily with the force of the law on those who continued to operate was largely successful, despite the shortcomings of the amnesty when viewed as a demobilisation, disarmament and reintegration (DDR) programme.

Niger Delta militants

The amnesty followed a rise in attacks from late 2005 as MEND (Movement for the Emancipation of the Niger Delta) emerged as an alliance between militant groups across the

Delta. MEND's demands included a call for a return to the fiscal federalism of the 1960 constitution that allowed regions to retain 50 per cent of oil and other revenues, the withdrawal of oil companies from Nigeria and the release of key prisoners from the Ijaw ethnic group. That was the immediate context that guided the President Umaru Musa Yar'Adua led federal government to inaugurate the amnesty programme. The amnesty was largely successful, however:[35]

1. While the amnesty programme successfully paid off ex-militants with training and stipends, it was not able to provide them with jobs. The programme raised expectations that it was not able to meet, and these are catalysts for criminal activities among those unable to find work.

2. The amnesty package was not part of a broader peace-building strategy for the region. For stability to be sustainable beyond the amnesty, a comprehensive post-conflict reconciliation and peace building programme for the Niger Delta will be required as a priority.

3. A considerable volume of arms remain in circulation as the disarmament elements of the programme were weak.

4. Security provision is short-sighted and incoherent, which focused mainly on providing security for the oil industry rather than on broader human security.

5. The amnesty programme is not part of a coherent, well-designed and effectively implemented vision of development for the region.

---

35 This policy brief is based on a paper prepared for Nigeria Stability and Reconciliation Programme, (NSRP) by Kathryn Nwajiaku-Dahou, DPhil (Oxon). http://www.nsrp-nigeria. org/wp-content/uploads/2014/11/E189-NSRP-Policy-Brief-ND-Amnesty-4-Yrs-On_ FINAL_web.pd

6. Stakes in elections are very high as ex-militants can easily align with a preferred party or even candidate.

There were many militant groups in the Niger Delta that participated in the amnesty programme, including:

i.   Movement for the Emancipation of the Niger Delta (MEND)
ii. Niger Delta Liberation Front (NDLF)
iii. Niger Delta People's Volunteer Force (NDPVF)
iv. Niger Delta Vigilante (NDV)

Six years after the inauguration of the amnesty programme, a new militant group, **The Niger Delta Avengers (NDA)** emerged. **The Niger Delta Avengers** became "public" in January 2016, seven months after the inauguration of President Muhammadu Buhari. The NDA espouse the following military and political objectives:

- Cripple the Nigerian economy ('Operation Red Economy');
- Force the government to negotiate the demands in a 'sovereign national conference;'
- Re-allocation of Nigerian ownership of oil blocs (in favour of Niger Deltans);
- Autonomy/self-determination for the Niger Delta.

Their strategies and patterns of attack suggest that they are few but well-trained. They claimed on their website to be young, educated and well-travelled. They say they are better armed and more civilised than past militants. On Thursday, June 9, 2016 they issued the following statement:

ENOUGH OF THIS INJUSTICE

Since the day crude oil was discovered in commercial quantity and quality in Oloibiri, present day Bayelsa

State, what we have been asking from successive governments in Nigeria is potable drinking water in the midst of plenty of water mass, electricity, roads, employment, quality education/educational facilities, resource control, participation in the oil business and inclusive governance that will engender substantial freedom.

The reverse has been the case, from Oloibiri, Brass LNLG and export terminals in Bayelsa; Bonny LNLG and export terminals in River state; Exxon Mobil in Akwa Ibom; Escravos EGTL/ Tankfarm and export terminals; Forcados Tankfarm and export terminals in Delta State operated respectively by Anglo-Dutch Shell, Chevron/Texaco Over seas, Agip ENI, Exxon Mobil. The history of the communal lives is terror of poverty, inhumanity and desolate living conditions. But when you move into these facilities operated by the Multinational Oil Corporations, they are living like kings and presidents.

For over five decades, we have given multinational oil corporations and their collaborators, the Nigerian State, peace, cooperation and love for the crude oil to flow unhindered from our land. The continuous tranquility is only manifesting in the development of mountains, rocks, valleys, deserts and lagoons but the Niger Delta territory is continually alienated from all types of development and all essence of quality human life. Meanwhile, all successive governments worship the crude oil taken from the region. Our communities and the people are only good at securing the pipelines, oil and gas facilities. What a tragedy?

We are calling on the international community especially Britain, France, the United States of America, Russia, China and European Union to speak up against this ongoing terror and come to the aid of the Niger Delta, as witnesses to this grave inhumanity and history of terror perpetuated against the people of the Niger Delta daily. This history of terror, we the Niger Delta Avengers will resist and correct with every means necessary. We have nothing to lose in the battles ahead; justice they say is only found within the structure of a nation state. Rather than provide this justice, the Nigerian government has decided to mobilise her military might to intimidate, torture, maim, victimise and bombard a section of the nation state and her citizenry to allow the free flow of our oil.

Some persons, groups, and commentators may ask, what do the people of the Niger Delta want? We are not like some of these personalities who run champagne parties or turn Rivers State Government House into a house patrimony of god-sons and prebendalism. They say the progress and success of a nation state is the reflection of her constitution that is not manufactured to favour some sections and exclude the yearning and aspirations of others; but the indwelling spiritual and historical development of its people.

Since the amalgamation of Nigeria in 1914 to date, our resources have been used to sustain the political, administrative live wire of Nigeria to the exclusion of the Niger Delta.

Finally, we are calling on the international community to come and support the restoration of our right to peaceful self-determination from this tragedy of 1914 that has expired since 2014. We want our resources back to restore the essence of human life in our region for generations to come because Nigeria has failed to do that. The world should not wait until we go the Sudan ways. Enough is enough God Bless Niger Delta People.

Nigerians can no longer take refuge in silence; these issues as raised by NDA are realistic and pathetic. The ethnic structure of Nigerian politics has blinded our politicians from making realistic effort to correct these anomalies and some Nigerian leaders are not educated enough to appreciate the enormity of the harm done.

10

FUNDAMENTAL ISSUES IN THE NIGER DELTA REGION

Oil violence in the Niger Delta region revolves around some salient fundamental issues, which the Nigerian State has not summoned even the much-needed political will to tackle since crude oil was struck in 1956. Oil and environmental violence are rooted in the inequitable social relations that undergird the production and distribution of profits from oil, and its adverse impact on the fragile ecosystem of the Niger Delta. This involves the Nigerian State and oil companies on one side, and the people of the oil-producing communities of Niger Delta on the other side.

In contention is the oil-rich environment, the manner of distributing its wealth, and the survival of its inhabitants who depend on the ecosystem for their basic needs and livelihood. The host communities contend that because the oil is mined in their land, and that they suffer from the pollution and environmental degradation attendant to oil production, they therefore have the right to adequate compensation, clean environment, and a fair share of oil rents, while the state and its partners, the oil multinationals, insist on the optimisation of rents and profits on the basis of modalities defined exclusively by the patronage.[36]

---

36 Cyril Obi, Oil, "Environmental Conflict and National Security in Nigeria: Ramifications of the Ecology-Security Nexus for Sub-Regional Peace. *Program in Arms Control, Disarmament, and International Security Arms Control and Disarmament and International Security Program*, University of Illinois at Urbana–Champaign, January 1997" in https://www.ideals. illinois.edu/bitstream/handle/2142/18/ObiOP

Environmental Pollution and Despoliation

Oil spills often result in both immediate and long-term environmental damage. Some of the environmental damages caused by an oil spill can last for decades after the spill had occurred. Oil spilled by damaged tankers, pipelines or offshore oil rigs coats everything it touches and becomes an unwelcome but long-term part of every ecosystem it enters. When an oil slick from a large oil spill reaches the beach, the oil coats and clings to every rock and grain of sand. Also, if the oil washes into coastal marshes, mangrove forests or other wetlands, fibrous plants and grasses absorb the oil, which could damage the plants and make the whole area unsuitable as wildlife habitat.

Oil spill

Oil prospecting and exploration operations also pollute the underground water and the environment, especially through the process of cuttings and reinjection used for several years by some drilling waste management companies. Several waste management companies deceitfully dump the wastes into rivers, seas and the environment, while giving the impression that they were reinjected into old oil wells.

Moreso, there is a high level of farmland and aquatic species destruction. The people of the Niger Delta who were originally farmers and fishermen, have their means of livelihood destroyed; as there is loss of fertile farmland, decline in agricultural produce, migration, loss and destruction of aquatic resources, contamination of other natural sources as well as drinking water, atmospheric pollution, rapid corrosion of roofing sheets (acid rain), gradual extinction and migration of wildlife, general biodiversity destruction and massive rural/urban migration. Oil exploration and production has led to environmental damage on many levels: land, water and air pollution, depleted fishing grounds and the disappearance of wetlands.[37]

Gas flaring

These environmental changes have had significant implications on local livelihoods, and the alienation of people from their resources and land. Measures to counterbalance environmental damage are inadequate and this is a major focus of community discontent in the Niger Delta.

---

37   World Bank and Department for International Development (2005) 'Country Partnership Strategy for the Federal Republic of Nigeria (2005-2009): Washington DC: World Bank.

Legislations of Disempowerment and Subjugation

Many people in the Niger Delta blame their poverty on two federal laws: the 1969 Petroleum Act, which gave the state sole ownership and control of the country's oil and gas reserves; and the Land Use Act of 1978 which makes the government the owner of all land in Nigeria. Many activists in the Niger Delta say oil companies should pay rents and royalties for the use of the land directly to land owners and to local communities instead of the central government. They are also calling for a return to Nigeria's 1960 constitution which calls for revenue to be shared equally between federal and local governments. But they say the Land Act has undermined efforts by individuals and communities to get compensation when their land is requisitioned for oil activities or when oil companies pollute the land.

The realisation that oil is a veritable source of wealth and the fact that it is found in the part of Nigeria largely inhabited by the southern minorities, spurred the Nigerian State into the promulgation of some questionable legislations, like Decree No. 51 of 1969, which was used to transfer the ownership of the totality of petroleum products in the Niger Delta region to the federal government of Nigeria; and the Land Use Decree of 1978, which also vested land ownership in Nigeria in the Federal Government and its accredited agents; thereby dispossessed the Niger Delta people of ownership and occupancy rights to their oil rich lands. These laws are systematically deployed as instruments of subjugation, domination and expropriation of the Delta resources by the Nigerian State.

There is much juridical ambiguity over land rights. While the Land Use Decree of 1978 formally vested all land in state governments, the expropriation of this has never been accepted by the individuals, families and communities that have made customary claims to the land. This led to a double system, and combined with weak judicial systems has resulted in long running conflicts and ambiguity at many levels.

Politics of Marginalisation and Exclusion

Marginality is an experience that affects millions of people and many communities in the Niger Delta. People who are marginalised have relatively little control over their lives, and the resources available to them. This results in making them handicapped in contributing positively to the society. A vicious circle is set up whereby their lack of positive and supportive relationships means that they are prevented from participating in local life, which in turn leads to further isolation. This has tremendous impact on the development of human beings, as well as on the society at large. As the objective of development is to create an enabling environment for people to enjoy a productive, healthy, and creative life, it is important to address the issue of marginalisation in the Niger Delta.

A marginalised Niger Delta community

Despite the significant natural resource endowments and the substantial resource flows to the federal government, the people of the Niger Delta are destitute. They feel excluded from the wealth generated by their resource rich region. Oil wealth, from the Niger Delta region, is largely responsible for sustaining the Nigerian Federation (UNDP, 2006:62). Despite contributing greatly to Nigeria's economic growth, the Niger Delta is somewhat marginalised from Nigeria's national development. Essentially, there is a significant disconnect between the wealth the region generates for the Nigerian Federation and the transnational oil companies extracting oil from the region, and the region's human development progress. The principle of derivation, which was hitherto based on fifty per cent resource allocation to region (state) of origin, was abrogated. Rather, new variables suddenly sprang up as the bases for the allocation of resources to states. This was obviously to the detriment of the socio-economic development of the Niger Delta region and its people.

Social and Political Exclusion

The people of Niger Delta are politically disadvantaged as elections in the Niger Delta states are widely agreed to have been extensively rigged, with fraudulent results sustained by violence and threat and so leaving a serious democratic deficit. The political process is held in complete mistrust and considered exclusionary and corrupt. Hence, formal institutions have failed to be of any help just as the local customary institutions have become eroded. Youths have turned violent and have become militants to challenge the government and extort oil and money from oil companies. Corruption, especially at the state and local levels, is endemic and is the root of many of the region's problems. Large sums are received at both the state and local government levels, but there is little evidence that this is being applied to productive development endeavours. This situation exacerbates the sense of hopelessness, exclusion and anger of the citizenry of the Niger Delta, who have lost faith in the existing governance structures.[38]

Conflict has become militarised, with the intensive proliferation of arms, sabotage, hostage taking and the emergence of warlords and youth cults. This process is fuelled by the illegal bunkering of oil fuels fields.[39] The democratisation of the means of violence has emerged, as the state has lost monopoly of power over the use of force. This violence has emerged in many forms, between (a) communities over host community status, resource, land claims and surveillance contracts; (b) within communities over compensation distribution; (c) between communities and oil companies; and (d) between communities and security forces.

Persistent conflict, while in part is a response to the region's poor human development, also serves to entrench this poverty. The major reason for the discontent in the Niger Delta and in the militants is that there is no genuine political process. Elections have been notorious in their failure to reflect the will of the people. In turn, there is little incentive for the development of broad-based political parties or movements. The long-term prospects for peace and prosperity in the Niger Delta depend upon true electoral reform and the development of popular political parties and institutions through which popular will can be expressed and protected. One role the international community could play would be to help build the capacity in the Niger Delta for an effective political movement just

---

38   UN Integrated Regional Information Networks (2007) 'Nigeria: New Hope for Old 'Master Plan' on Niger Delta', allAfrica.com, http://allafrica.com/stories/200711191052.html (21 November 2007).

39   World Bank (2007) 'Nigeria Country Brief. Washington: World Bank. http://web.worldbank. org/WBSITE/EXTERNAL/COUNTRIES/AFRICAEXT/NIGERIAEXTN/0, menuPK:36890 6~pagePK:141132~piPK:141107~theSitePK:36889 6,00.html

like the international community did in South Africa in the 1980s and early 1990s.

The Land Is Ours

There were different land tenure systems in almost every part of the Niger Delta and every part of Nigeria before the Land Use Act. However, what was common in almost all the systems was their dependence on the custom and the customary law of the people. In most parts of the Niger Delta, particularly in Ikwerre, the administration of land was carried out under the customary tenure. Land ownership was defined by families, villages and clans.

From time immemorial, through the period of agriculture, to the period of industrial development, land has remained the most valuable property in the life of people and their development. Land is a source of wealth to those who have it and the mother of all properties. Virtually all the basic needs of human existence are land-dependent. In view of the importance and usefulness of land, every person generally desires to acquire and own a portion of land.

Prior to colonial era, host communities were involved in decisions and were partakers in the benefits that accrues from trade in their kingdom, and resources were utilised for the benefits of the community in question. However, the colonialists declared, upon arrival, that the land they were to settle was a *Terra Nullius*, a no man's land.

The Constitution of the Federal Republic of Nigeria 1999, Section 44(3), vests the ownership and control of all minerals, mineral oils and natural gas in, under or upon any land in Nigeria, its territorial waters, and exclusive economic zone on the federal government, and the federal government is to manage such minerals in such manner as may be prescribed by the National Assembly.

Thus, the constitution confers exclusive jurisdiction on the National Assembly on matters relating to oil, gas and other minerals. This provision is an adoption of a series of statutory laws and regulations promulgated by the Federal Military Government between 1969 and 1990.

The Land Use Act was enacted and enshrined into the constitution of Nigeria without due respect to customs and cultures regulating land. It was capriciously injected into the constitution for selfish reasons by those who are by no means experts in land law without provisions for the respectability of the environment. The Land Use Decree (now Land Use Act) was promulgated on 29th of March, 1978 following the recommendations of a minority report of a panel appointed by the Federal Military Government of the time to advise on future land policy. With immediate effect, it vested all land in each state of the federation in the governor of that state. The Act vests all land comprised in the territory of each state (except land vested in the federal government for its agencies) solely in the hands of the governors of the state who would hold such land in trust for the people.

The promulgation of the Petroleum Act of 1969 marked a watershed in the history of petroleum legislation in Nigeria. It stipulated for the first time that the entire ownership and control of all petroleum in Nigeria is vested in the Federal Government of Nigeria. The Act vested the entire ownership and control of oil and gas resources in, under or upon all land or territorial waters in the Nigerian Government, and authorises the Federal Ministry of Petroleum Resources to issue licenses to Nigerian citizens or companies incorporated in Nigeria for oil prospecting, drilling, production, storage, refining, and transportation activities. The Exclusive Economic Zone Act 1978 also vests on the Federal Government of Nigeria sovereign and exclusive rights with respect to the exploration and exploitation of the natural resources of the seabed, sub-soil and superjacent waters of the Exclusive Economic Zone.

The people of Ikwerre and almost every other ethnic group in the Niger Delta see the Land Use Act as a foreign law. The European concepts about land and property differ from those of Nigeria in two important ways. First, under European law, land is a commodity that could be bought and sold, and individuals who "owned" a tract of land had, for the most part, exclusive rights to its use. Second, ownership is determined by formal means, recognised by deeds or contracts that are also enforced by courts of law. Our colonialists, used to monarchy, often assumed wrongly that the chief of a village could sell land on behalf of his people, when in fact his powers were far more limited. The Europeans also assumed that every piece of land must either have a single owner or ruler, when in fact, most land in Niger Delta was shared in many ways.

Land rights are more complicated in the cultures of the Niger Delta People. A family might "own" the land on which its house stood, while individuals "own" the land on which they farm. But homes, agricultural fields, and villages move frequently, so land is only "owned" as long as it is being used. Villages collectively have rights to large territories that they use for hunting, fishing, and gathering of food, medicinal herbs, and raw materials for building or tools. The rights shift depending on the use and the people using it. For most purposes, all the people in a village share the use of its land. Among different villages, agreements about land are made and defended. A village might claim exclusive hunting rights in a given territory, for example, but people from many villages might share the use of a single river for fishing. What villages claim is "not the land but the things that are on the land during the various seasons of the year."

Presently, the oil industry in Nigeria is operating on the foreign principle that informed the Land Use Act. The oil industry culture, in the observation of Professor I.E. Sagay, is founded on five assumptions:[40]

i.   That profit maximisation is the only basis upon which a company can be run, so that any expenditure beyond what is required to get out the oil is resisted;

ii. That a "deal" can be made with government only, regardless of the government's legality or morality, and regardless also of the wishes or needs of the local people;

iii. That once an arrangement has been made with a government, a mining company can do what it likes – in fact, it can act as if it is a government agency;

iv. That the "market" (i.e., the industrialised world) has a right to have the resources it wants, at the lowest possible price, and regardless of the costs to the local people who are obliged to play host to mining companies; and

v.   That "we", the mining companies, know best and are acting responsibly.

Kekong Bisong in his studies of P. Oluyede's *Nigerian Law of Conveyancing* has made a compelling presentation that in all parts of Nigeria, customary land law was and still is recognised. In the Northern States, customary interests in land are not only recognised but are safeguarded under the Land and Native Rights Ordinance, now replaced as

---

40   Professor I.E. Sagay, *"Human Rights, Justice and the Niger Delta: Issues and Challenges"* http://www.profitsesagay.com/

amended by the Land Tenure Law of 1962.[41] In the rest of the federation, the existing customary law is also being preserved.

Practically speaking, most Nigerians live in the rural areas and the bulk of their rural land is governed exclusively (or almost) by customary law, just as in pre-colonial days. Land occupies a central position in the rural communities as well as in the urban cities, and the customs regulating its tenure are deeply entrenched in their social and cultural life.[42]

It has been observed that some of the major causes of the Niger Delta conflicts are particularly consequences of attempts to combine two or all of the above notions of land law in a single transaction involving customary land tenure. In the pre-colonial Nigeria and after the reception of English law as part of the Nigerian legal system, land was and is still subject to incidents of native law and custom. The Land Use Act,[43] did not in any way abolish or abrogate rights and interests existing under customary land law. In our culture and within our customary law, a community that own land own everything above the land up to the heavens and down to the innermost depths of the earth. This is the basis of the contention with the Land Use Act.

Other laws that infringe on the rights of the Niger Delta people include:

1. Section 2 (1) of the Environmental Impact Assessment Act Cap E12 LFN 2004.

2. Mineral and Mining Act, Cap. M12 LFN 2004 – (i) Section 1 (1) - vests the entire property in the Government of the Federation. (ii) Section 2 (c) –

---

41   P.A. OLUYEDE, *Nigerian Law of Conveyancing*, (Ibadan, Ibadan University Press, 1978), 6.
42   *Ibid.*
43   Land Use Act, Cap. 202, L.F.N., 1990.

the Minister should monitor the development and exploration of all minerals considered strategic.

3. The Niger Delta Development Commission Act, Cap 86 LFN 2004 – (i) Section 7 - stipulates the functions and powers of the commission. (ii) Section 8 – vests the power to control the commission in a board. (iii) Section 14 – stipulates the funding for the commission. (iv) Section 21 – establishes a Monitoring Committee.

4. The Petroleum Act, P10 LFN 2004.

5. Allocation of Revenue (Abolition of Dichotomy in the Application of Derivation) Act LFN 2004.

6. The Land Use Act L5 LFN 2004.

7. Oil Pipeline Act O7 LFN 2004.

8. The Exclusive Economic Zone Act Cap E17 LFN 2004.

9. National Inland Waterways Act Cap N47 LFN 2004.

10. Land (Title Vesting, etc.) Act L7 LFN, 2004.

11. Territorial Waters Act CapT15 LFN, 2004.

12. Interpretation Act Cap I23 LFN, 2004.

13. Environmental Guidelines and Standards for the Petroleum Industry in Nigeria, 1991.

14. Petroleum (Drilling and Production) Regulations, 1969.

15. Harmful Waste (Special Criminal Provisions, etc.) Act Cap H1 LFN, 2004.

16. National Environment Protection (Effluent Limitation) Regulations, 1991.

17. Mineral Oils Safety Regulations, 1962.

18. Oil and Gas Pipelines Regulations, 1995.

19. National Environmental Protection (Pollution Abatement in Industries and Facilities Generating Wastes) Regulations, 1991.

20. National Environmental Standards and Regulations Enforcement Agency (Establishment) Act, 2007.

21. Oil in Navigable Waters Act Cap 06 LFN, 2004.

22. Nigeria Extractive Industries Transparency Initiative Act, 2007.

23. Independent Corrupt Practices and Related Offences Act, 2000.

24. Economic and Financial Crimes Commission (Establishment, etc.) Act Cap E1 LFN, 2004.

25. Crude Oil (Transportation and Shipment) Regulations, Cap Petroleum Act, LFN.

26. Agricultural (Control of Importation) Act Cap A13, LFN, 2004.

27. Associated Gas Re-Injection Act Cap A25, LFN, 2004.

28. Natural Resources Conservation Agency Council Act Cap 286, 1990.

29. Federal Environmental Protection Agency Act Cap F10, LFN, 2004 131, 1990.

30. Endangered Species (Control of International Trade and Traffic) Act E9, LFN, 2004.

31. Forest Ordinance, 1937.

32. Petroleum Profit Tax Act Cap P13 2004.

33. Petroleum Equalization (Management Board, etc.) Act Cap P14 2004.

34. Petroleum (Special Trust Fund) Act Cap P14 2004.

35. Oil Terminal Dues Act Cap 08 2004.

36. NNPC Act.

37. Special Petroleum Offensive Miscellaneous Decree.

38. Sea Fisheries Act Cap S4 2004.

11

THE QUEST FOR JUSTICE BY COMMUNITIES

Most people in the Niger Delta may not have heard of the term environmental injustice before. It is just a new word for an old problem. Environmental justice is based on the principle that all people have the right to be protected from environmental pollution and to live in and enjoy a clean and healthful environment. Environmental justice is the equal protection and meaningful involvement of all people in the development, implementation and enforcement of environmental laws, regulations and policies as well as the equitable distribution of environmental benefits.

Environmental injustice has existed for long, when the fact is considered that it is mostly the prosperous and wealthy people who have access to good water, good housing, good protection, good environment and overall, good and healthy lifestyle, while the poor live in detrimental conditions which eventually lead to multiple deprivations. This pattern has been seen commonly over the ages in most places and societies, such that it has been accepted to be like any other natural phenomenon. It is only in recent past that environmental justice has found a voice and is trying to address these issues.

It is however very clear that environmental injustices exist in the Niger Delta. It is impossible to eradicate these injustices all of a sudden, but it must be acknowledged that something has to be done in the future regarding this. So what can we do to prevent environmental injustice and to bring about true environmental justice? The first thing would be to make ourselves aware of the issues facing the Niger Delta today that are instances of environmental injustice. Next would be to get involved. This is why there have been several demands and petitions from ethnic nationalities and communities in the Niger Delta seeking attention from government and other interest groups that are operating in the region even though some of the groups have produced charters, declarations, agenda and resolutions to express their demands. These began with the Ogoni Bill of Rights in 1990; the Kaiama Declaration by the Niger Delta youths which contains reasons they want their resources; the Oron Bill of Rights in which the Oron people of Akwa Ibom State resolved to take their destiny into their own hands; and the Warri Accord in which the Itsekiri people of Delta State sought ways to maximally benefit from the oil production that is taking place in their area.

The Ogoni Bill of Rights, 1990

The people of Ogoni are considered by many as the pioneer of the Niger Delta struggle with the government of Nigeria and the oil companies: especially Shell Company where they maintain their rights as the original inhabitants of the land. The non-violent Movement for the Survival of the Ogoni People (MOSOP) was led by its president, Ken Saro-Wiwa. Ken Saro-Wiwa was a well-known environmental activist, author, and Nobel Peace Prize nominee who coordinated the publication of the Ogoni Bill of Rights in 1990. The bill highlighted the Ogoni people's lack of social services, their political marginalisation, and the maltreatment they faced from the Shell Oil Company. The bill demanded environmental protection for the Ogoni region, self-determination for the Ogoni nation, cultural rights for the Ogoni people, representation in Nigerian institutions, and a fair proportion of the revenue from the sale of the region's oil. The key demands of the bill are itemised thus:

- Political control of Ogoni affairs by Ogoni people;
- The right to control and use a fair proportion of Ogoni's economic resources for Ogoni development;
- Adequate and direct representation of the Ogoni people as a matter of right in all Nigerian national institutions;
- The use and development of the Ogoni language in Ogoni territory;
- The full development of Ogoni culture;
- The right to religious freedom for its people; and
- The right to protect the Ogoni environment and ecology from further degradation.

The Ogoni Bill of Rights generated national and international interests which led to a non-violent protests by the indigenous people of Ogoni. Notwithstanding the huge international attention the campaign attracted, all MOSOP activities were non-violent, although angry protesters beat one Shell employee in January 1993. After the January 4 action and further protests throughout the month, Shell Oil pulled out of the region. With shell oil out, this drastically lowered the amount of crude oil that is extracted from the region and further reduced the profit of the oil companies operating in the area by 200 million dollars in 1993.

In response to the First Ogoni Day's success and Shell's withdrawal, the unstable national government decided to forcefully suppress Ogoni activities. Ken Saro-Wiwa and eight other activists were hanged in Port Harcourt prison on

November 10, 1995, with riot police and tanks overseeing the execution.

This gruesome hanging of Dr. Ken Saro-Wiwa and eight other people is the worst pastoral hazard in my thirty-three years as a Catholic priest. I was an eyewitness to the execution of the nine Ogoni people. I also had the privilege of praying for them and Nigeria before their death. In response to the killings and ongoing oppression of the Ogoni people, that same day, Nigeria was suspended from the Commonwealth of Nations. This suspension was encouraged by Nelson Mandela who represented South Africa in the Commonwealth. Supporters of the Ogoni people held protest marches at Nigerian embassies and Shell offices around the world. Many world leaders called for an oil embargo, economic sanctions, and bans on arms sales. Groups such as Amnesty International and Greenpeace held protest actions as well. The International Finance Corporation, which had proposed a $100 million loan and $80 million equity deal to produce a gas plant and pipeline in the Niger Delta cancelled its proposal following the executions.

OGONI BILL OF RIGHTS
PRESENTED TO THE GOVERNMENT AND
PEOPLE OF NIGERIA, NOVEMBER 1990

We, the people of Ogoni (Babbe, Gokana, Ken Khana, Nyo Khan and Tai) numbering about 500,000, being a separate and distinct ethnic nationality within the Federal Republic of Nigeria, wish to draw the attention of the government and people of Nigeria to the undermentioned facts:
1. That the Ogoni people, before the advent of British colonialism, were not conquered or colonised by any other ethnic group in present day Nigeria.

2. That British colonisation forced us into the administrative division of Opobo from 1908 to 1947.

3. That we protested against this forced union until the Ogoni Native Authority was created in 1947 and placed under the then Rivers Province.

4. That in 1951, we were forcibly included in the Eastern Region of Nigeria where we suffered utter neglect.

5. That we protested against this neglect by voting against the party in power in the region in 1957, and against the forced union by testimony before the Willink Commision of Inquiry into Minority Fears in 1958.

6. That this protest led to the inclusion of our nationality in Rivers state in 1967, which state consists of several ethnic nationalities with differing cultures, languages and aspirations.

7. That oil was struck and produced in commercial quantities on our land in 1958 at K. Dere (Bomu oilfield).

8. That oil has been mined on our land since 1958 to this day from the following oilfields: (i) Bomu (ii) Bodo West (iii) Tai (iv) Korokoro (v) Yorla (vi) Lubara Creek and (vii) Afam by Shell Petroleum Development Company (Nigeria) Limited.

9. That in over 30 years of oil mining, the Ogoni nationality has provided the Nigerian nation with a total revenue estimated at over 40 billion naira (₦40 billion) or 30 billion dollars.

10. That in return for the above contribution, the Ogoni people have received nothing.

11. That today, the Ogoni people have:

     i.   No representation whatsoever in ALL institutions of the Federal Government of Nigeria;

    ii.   No pipe-borne water;

   iii.   No electricity;

   iv.   No job opportunities for the citizens in federal, state, public sector or private sector companies;

    v.   No social or economic project of the federal government.

12. That the Ogoni languages of Gokana and Khana are undeveloped and are about to disappear, whereas other Nigerian languages are being forced on us.

13. That the ethnic policies of successive federal and state governments are gradually pushing the Ogoni people to slavery and possible extinction.

14. That the Shell Petroleum Development Company of Nigeria Limited does not employ Ogoni people at a meaningful or any level at all, in defiance of the federal government's regulations.

15. That the search for oil has caused severe land and food shortages in Ogoni – one of the most densely populated areas of Africa (average: 1,500 per square mile; national average: 300 per square mile).

16. That neglectful environmental pollution laws and sub-standard inspection techniques of the federal authorities have led to the complete degradation of the Ogoni environment, turning our homeland into an ecological disaster.

17. That the Ogoni people lack education, health and other social facilities.

18. That it is intolerable that one of the richest areas of Nigeria should wallow in abject poverty and destitution.

19. That successive federal administrators have trampled on every minority right enshrined in the Nigerian Constitution to the detriment of the Ogoni and have by administrative structuring and other noxious acts transferred Ogoni wealth exclusively to other parts of the republic.

20. That the Ogoni people wish to manage their own affairs.

Now therefore, while reaffirming our wish to remain a part of the Federal Republic of Nigeria, we make demand upon the republic as follows:

That the Ogoni people be granted POLITICAL AUTONOMY to participate in the affairs of the republic as a distinct and separate unit by whatever name called, provided that this autonomy guarantees the following:

a. Political control of Ogoni affairs by Ogoni people.

b. The right to the control and use of a fair proportion of OGONI economic resources for Ogoni development.

c. Adequate and direct representation as of right in all Nigerian national institutions.

d. The use and development of Ogoni languages in Ogoni territory.

e. The full development of Ogoni culture.

f. The right to religious freedom.

g. The right to protect the Ogoni environment and ecology from further degradation.

We make the above demands in the knowledge that it does not deny any other ethnic group in the Nigerian

Federation their rights and that it can only conduce to peace, justice and fair play and hence, stability and progress in the Nigerian nation.

We make the above demands in the belief that, as Obafemi Awolowo has written: "In a true Federation, each ethnic group, no matter how small; is entitled to the same treatment as any other ethnic group, no matter how large."

We demand these rights as equal members of the Nigerian Federation who contribute and have contributed to the growth of the federation and have a right to expect full returns from that federation.

Adopted by general acclaim of the Ogoni people on the 26th day of August, 1990, at Bori, Rivers State.

The Charter of Demands of the Ogbia People, 1992

On 1st November 1992, the Ogbia people, host to Nigeria's first commercial oil well, the Oloibiri oil field, expressed their dissent over the state of affairs in their community, particularly their lack of development, by petitioning the federal government through a general proclamation entitled, **'The Charter of Demands of the Ogbia People.'** The document affirmed the people's willingness to remain an integral part of the country but raised specific demands on the country. It asked the federal government to:

1. Declare Ogbia as a disaster area needing national emergency assistance particularly in form of social infrastructure and economic development;

2. Repeal laws which are inimical to the people's rights to the resources in the land. These are laws such as the Petroleum Act of 1969, the Land Use Decree, 1978, and aspects of the then 1989 Constitution;

3. Pay to them royalties and rents from oil exploration;

4. Pay to them a specified amount of $35.5 billion to restore their environment and for future investment to protect the environment;

5. Apply the derivation principle of 50% to the people's resources;

6. Engage in fair appointment and employment of the people of Ogbia in national institutions;

7. End gas flaring;

8. Build the Oloibiri oil museum, which foundation had earlier been laid, and construct shore protection for communities suffering from erosion menace.

The Kaiama Declaration, 1998

On 11 December 1998, youths from different clans, together with representatives from political organisations from Ijaw, gathered together in Kaiama, a town in the Kolokuma/ Opokuma Local Government Area (LGA) of Bayelsa State. After prayer, speeches and much deliberation, delegates issued the Kaiama Declaration:

- That all minerals within their territories should be controlled by Ijaw people;

- That laws which deprive people of the resources under their soil are undemocratic and should not be obeyed;

- That the military should be redeployed away from Ijaw territories;

- That oil companies should cease to explore oil in their lands, given the prevailing atmosphere of gas flaring, oil spillages, etc.;

- That there should be a Sovereign National Conference (SNC) with representation based on equality of ethnic nationalities;
- The SNC is to discuss the basis for the co-existence of the various ethnic nationalities in the country.

THE KAIAMA DECLARATION
BY
IJAW YOUTHS OF THE NIGER DELTA
BEING THE COMMUNIQUE ISSUED AT THE
END OF THE ALL IJAW YOUTHS CONFERENCE
WHICH HELD IN THE TOWN OF KAIAMA THIS
DAY OF DECEMBER 1998.

INTRODUCTION

We, Ijaw youths drawn from over five hundred communities from over 40 clans that make up the Ijaw nation and representing 25 representative organisations met today, in Kaiama to deliberate on the best way to ensure the continuous survival of the indigenous peoples of the Ijaw ethnic nationality of the Niger Delta within the Nigerian state.

After exhaustive deliberations, the conference observed:

a. That it was through British colonisation that the IJAW NATION was forcibly put under the Nigerian State.

b. That but for the economic interests of the imperialists, the Ijaw ethnic nationality would have evolved as a distinct and separate sovereign nation, enjoying undiluted political, economic, social, and cultural AUTONOMY.

c. That the division of the Southern Protectorate into East and West in 1939 by the British marked the beginning of the balkanisation of a hitherto territorially contiguous and culturally homogeneous Ijaw people into political and administrative units, much to our disadvantage. This trend is continuing in the balkanisation of the Ijaws into six states – Ondo, Edo, Delta, Bayelsa, Rivers and Akwa Ibom States, mostly as minorities who suffer socio-political, economic, cultural and psychological deprivations.

d. That the quality of life of Ijaw people is deteriorating as a result of utter neglect, suppression and marginalisation visited on Ijaws by the alliance of the Nigerian state and transnational oil companies.

e. That the political crisis in Nigeria is mainly about the struggle for the control of oil mineral resources which account for over 80% of GDP, 95% of national budget and 90% of foreign exchange earnings. From which, 65%, 75% and 70% respectively are derived from within the Ijaw nation. Despite these huge contributions, our reward from the Nigerian State remains avoidable deaths resulting from ecological devastation and military repression.

f. That the unbaiting damage done to our fragile natural environment and to the health of our people is due in the main to uncontrolled exploration and exploitation of crude oil and natural gas which has led to numerous oil spillages, uncontrolled gas flaring, the opening up of our forests to loggers, indiscriminate canalisation, flooding, land subsidence, coastal erosion, earth tremors, etc. Oil and gas are exhaustible resources and the complete lack of concern for ecological rehabilitation, in the light of the Oloibiri experience, is a signal of impending doom for the peoples of Ijaw land.

g. That the degradation of the environment of Ijaw land by transnational oil companies and the Nigerian State arises mainly because Ijaw people have been robbed of their natural rights to ownership and control of their land and resources through the instrumentality of undemocratic Nigerian State legislations such as the Land Use Decree of 1978, the Petroleum Decrees of 1969 and 1991, the Lands (Title Vesting etc.) Decree No. 52 of 1993 (Osborne Land Decree), the National Inland Waterways Authority Decree No. 13 of 199, etc.

h. That the principle of Derivation in Revenue Allocation has been consciously and systematically obliterated by successive regimes of the Nigerian State. We note the drastic reduction of the Derivation Principle from 100% (1953), 50% (1960), 45% (1970), 20% (1975) 2% (1982), 1.5% (1984) to 3% (1992 to date), and a rumoured 13% in Abacha's 1995 undemocratic and unimplemented constitution.

i. That the violence in Ijaw land and other parts of the Niger Delta area, sometimes manifesting in intra and inter ethnic conflicts are sponsored by the state and transnational oil companies to keep the communities of the Niger Delta area divided, weak and distracted from the causes of their problems.

j. That the recent revelations of the looting of national treasury by the Abacha junta is only a reflection of an existing and continuing trend of stealing by public office holders in the Nigerian State. We remember the over 12 billion dollars Gulf War windfall, which was looted by Babangida and his cohorts. We note that over 70% of the billions of dollars being looted by military rulers and their civilian collaborators is derived from our ecologically devastated Ijaw land.

Based on the foregoing, we, the youths of Ijaw land, hereby make the following resolutions to be known as the Kaiama Declaration:

• All land and natural resources (including mineral resources) within the Ijaw territory belong to Ijaw communities and are the basis of our survival.

- We cease to recognise all undemocratic decrees that rob our peoples/communities of the right to ownership and control of our lives and resources, which were enacted without our participation and consent. These include the Land Use Decree and The Petroleum Decree, etc.

- We demand the immediate withdrawal from Ijaw land of all military forces of occupation and repression by the Nigerian State. Any oil company that employs the services of the armed forces of the Nigerian State to "protect" its operations will be viewed as an enemy of the Ijaw people. Family members of military personnel stationed in Ijaw land should appeal to their people to leave the Ijaw area alone.

- Ijaw youths in all the communities in all Ijaw clans in the Niger Delta will take steps to implement these resolutions beginning from the 30th of December, 1998, as a step towards reclaiming the control of our lives. We, therefore, demand that all oil companies stop all exploration and exploitation activities in the Ijaw area. We are tired of gas flaring, oil spillages, blow outs and being labelled saboteurs and terrorists. It is a case of preparing the noose for our hanging. We reject this labelling. Hence, we advice all oil companies' staff and contractors to withdraw from Ijaw territories by the 30th December, 1998 pending the resolution of the issue of resource ownership and control in the Ijaw area of the Niger Delta.

- Ijaw youths and peoples will promote the principle of peaceful coexistence between all Ijaw communities and with our immediate neighbours, despite the provocative and divisive actions of the Nigerian State, transnational oil companies and their contractors. We offer a hand of friendship and comradeship to our neighbours: the Itsekiri, Ilaje, Urhobo, Isoko,

Edo, Ibibio, Ogoni, Ekpeye, Ikwerre, etc. We affirm our commitment to joint struggle with the other ethnic nationalities in the Niger Delta area for self-determination.

- We express our solidarity with all peoples, organisations and ethnic nationalities in Nigeria and elsewhere who are struggling for self-determination and justice. In particular, we note the struggle of the Oodua Peoples Congress (OPC), the Movement for the Survival of Ogoni People (MOSOP), Egi Women's Movement, etc.

- We extend our hand of solidarity to the Nigerian oil workers (NUPENG and PENGASSAN) and expect that they will see this struggle for freedom as a struggle for humanity.

- We reject the present transition to civil rule programme of the Abubakar regime, as it is not preceded by restructuring of the Nigerian Federation. The way forward is a Sovereign National Conference of equally represented ethnic nationalities to discuss the nature of a democratic federation of Nigerian ethic nationalities. The conference noted the violence and killings that characterised the last local government elections in most parts of the Niger Delta. The conference pointed out that these electoral conflicts are a manifestation of the undemocratic and unjust nature of the military transition programme. The conference affirmed therefore, that the military are incapable of enthroning true democracy in Nigeria.

- We call on all Ijaws to remain true to their Ijawness and to work for the total liberation of our people. You have no other true home but that which is in Ijaw land.

- We agree to remain within Nigeria but to demand and work for self government and resource control for the Ijaw people. The conference approved that the best way for Nigeria is a federation of ethnic nationalities. The federation should be run on the basis of equality and social justice.

- Finally, Ijaw youths resolve to set up the Ijaw Youth Council (IYC) to coordinate the struggle of Ijaw peoples for self-determination and justice.

Signed for the entire participants by:

FELIX TUODOLO

Resolution of First Urhobo Economic Summit, 1998

The first Urhobo Economic Summit was organised by the Urhobo Foundation, an affiliate of Urhobo Progress Union (UPU). The theme of the summit was **"Forty Years of Oil and Gas."** At the close of the meeting, a call to action was released with the following resolutions:

1. Immortalise the souls of the 1,063 Nigerian lives lost during the Ijerehe inferno by building a specialist hospital as a national monument at the site of the disaster;

2. Abolish the OMPADEC decree and replace it with legislation giving the oil-producing areas the right of exploitation and utilisation of all resources in their territory and the responsibility for the development and environmental protection of their ancestral lands;

3. Implement immediately and unconditionally the federal government policy which restricts employment of non-skilled labour entirely to indigenes of oil-producing areas and at least 70% of skilled labour also to indigenes;

4. Compel oil companies operating in the region to implement fully, a June 1994 policy on supporting indigenous contractors and providing employment to locals;

5. Direct oil companies in the region to increase the scholarship awards to indigenes in the oil-producing areas;

6. Establish an *Indigenes Recruitment Centre* to counter the use by other ethnic groups of the National Youth Service Corp (NYSC) posting to exclude young educated local workforce.

The Ikwerre Rescue Charter, 1999

The social and environmental costs of oil production have been extensive. They include destruction of wildlife and biodiversity, loss of fertile soil, pollution of air and drinking water, degradation of farmland and damage to aquatic ecosystems, all of which have caused serious health problems for the inhabitants of areas surrounding oil production. Pollution is caused by gas flaring, above ground pipeline leakage, oil waste dumping and oil spills. These were some of the reasons of the Ikwerre Charter that recognises the damage and devastation done to the Ikwerre environment by multi-nationals and state-owned companies operating in the oil, gas, chemical, agricultural and construction sectors. As a result, Ikwerre Youths Convention (IYC) agreed to raise a minimum standard of action which will involve the people of the region and govern the operations of privately owned companies. The convention called on the government and all stakeholders to:

- Recognise the unacceptable impact now and in the future of the continuous acquisition of its ancestral lands under the camouflage of state and national development;

- Desist from further forceful acquisition of Ikwerre lands by the government, its agencies or representatives, companies and also individual speculators in land;

- Make payment in form of reparation for all seized and stolen lands by both the Nigerian and Rivers State Governments;
- Abolish the Land Use Act (as amended) in 1978; The Petroleum Act (as amended) in 1969 and a host of other laws which are inimical to the control of land by the communities;
- Create an Ikwerre State (comprising of Port Harcourt, Obio/Akpor, Ikwerre and Emohua Local Government Areas).

IKWERRE RESCUE CHARTER

A Declaration Adopted at the All Ikwerre Youths Convention Held under the Auspices of Ikwerre Youths Convention (IYC) in the Historic Town of Elele (Omerele) in Ikwerre Local Government Area of Rivers State, Nigeria on 4th September, 1999

PREAMBLE

Long before the forced amalgamation of Northern and Southern Protectorates in 1914 by the British colonialists, Nigeria was and essentially remains a union of vibrant ethnic nationalities. The creation of a 12-state structure in May 1967, threw up pristine Nigerian nationalities, which older and larger dispensations had subjugated. The idea of state creation heightened the quest for self-assertion and recognition of the ethnic identities of previously disadvantaged nationalities within the Nigerian Federation. Based on the actual acts of discrimination and marginalisation within the Old Rivers State, the Ikwerre ethnic nationality was and remains deeply committed to the principle of self-determination and autonomy to preside over our own affairs within the Nigerian Federation.

115

Arising from the above facts therefore: We, the Youths of Ikwerre Ethnic Nationality, acting for ourselves and on behalf of our distinct ethnic nationality in Nigeria, with a population of 14 million persons, presently comprising Port Harcourt, Obio/Akpor, Ikwerre and Emohua Local Government Areas, do hereby make the following declarations to the people and government of the Federal Republic of Nigeria, and to the world;

That as a unique ethnic nationality, our medium of communication (Ikwerre) has been recognised within the Niger Delta and the Federation as a Nigerian language.

That about 60% of our land has been acquired in the last 100 years for purposes of "development," resulting in the sacking of several towns and villages. For example, Orominieke, Eligbam, Elieke (parts of "Bori Camp") etc., have not been given any form of compensation, in addition to the cruel destruction of centres of worship and tourism, holy lands, graves and forests.

That the predominant farming occupation of our people was dealt a decisive blow with the acquisition of Obomotu (later renamed Port Harcourt) by the British. Since then, our ethnic nationality has come under severe pressures as a result of unremitting land acquisition by governments, companies and individual speculators, resulting in unspeakable land alienation and socio-cultural dislocation that have now forced our young people into alcoholism, prostitution, unemployment, crime, etc.

That some of the lands pretentiously acquired for public use, have since been converted into private use by dubious government agents without adequate compensation, or reference to the original owners.

That articulate and influential Ikwerre personalities have been and are still being trailed, harassed and assassinated by faceless elements apparently enjoying official protection. This way, about 1,000 activists (including the renowned scholar, statesman and politician, Chief Senator (Dr.) Obi Wali, have been murdered in suspicious circumstances in the last 10 years.

That Chief Senator (Dr.) Wali was brutally murdered in the sanctuary of his bedroom on 6th April 1993, while agitating for self-determination and development of the Ikwerre Ethnic Nationality in particular and other nationalities, by officially commissioned assassins who are still enjoying immunity from prosecution.

That even now, stringent efforts are still being intensified by powerful cabals to balkanise our homogenous ethnic nationality with a view to reducing the Ikwerre people into expendable minorities in their God-given land.

That despite the fact that in a true federal system, larger ethnic groups should not swallow or subjugate smaller groups, no Ikwerre indigene has been appointed as either a minister, ambassador, presidential special adviser, presidential special assistant, chairman of a federal board/commission, university vice chancellor, governor, security chief or into related positions since we were forced into the Nigerian "Federation."

That the crude oil forcefully taken from Ikwerre land in the last forty years without any compensation is valued at Sixty Billion United State Dollars ($60 b).

That the mindless exploration and exploitation of crude oil on our ancestral lands have inflicted grave environmental, socio-cultural and economic pains on our people to the point of extinction.

That the continuation of these identified forms of exploitation, marginalisation, oppression, and group alienation amount to ethnic decontamination and deliberate exclusion of Ikwerre people from government and corporate institutions.

That the indigenous colonisers and their inside collaborators cleverly renamed parts of Rumuwoji community in Rebisi Kingdom, as 'Abonnema Wharf,' including the Kidney, Eagle and Isaka Islands from which further encroachments are still being made into the Ikwerre hinterland.

That gas flaring and rampant explosions at several oil locations have sacked several Ikwerre communities. An example is the devastating inferno at the Apara Flow Station operated by the Shell Petroleum Development Company Limited, which burnt down several villages, polluted the environment and reduced indigenes of these areas into internal refugees in peace time in the late 1960s.

That a complex network of oil pipelines and abandoned dry wells criss-cross the length and breath of Ikwerre land with attendant environmental degradation, including incessant oil blow-outs.

Today, we the Ikwerre Youths, drawn from all the villages, towns, clans and those in the diaspora, gathered under the auspices of the Ikwerre Youths Convention (IYC), determined to take our destiny in our own hands, and to free ourselves from over a century-long entrapment and enslavement, repression and exploitation in the present Nigerian Federation, wish to openly and boldly publicise our cause.

Declarations

Conscious of the damages and devastation done to our environment by the multinational and state owned companies in the oil, gas, chemical, agricultural and construction industries through many years of exploitation and exploration of our natural and mineral resources, we hereby demand that all affected institutions should stop operations in Ikwerre land with immediate effect, in their own interests. Realising the impact now and in the future of the continuous acquisition of our ancestral lands under the camouflage of state and national development; knowing the number of such hectares of land seized for about 100 years, which financial value runs into billions of dollars and the negative effects of such unregulated acquisition of our only source of economic well-being and its attendant impact on us and our future generations in relation to the erosion of our culture and the calculated extinction of our ethnic group, we hereby re-assert our right to existence and dignity as clearly specified in the United Nations Universal Declaration on Human Rights and the African Charter on Peoples and Human Rights, particularly as they affect the protection of vulnerable indigenous tribes, we state as follows:

1. That no further forceful acquisition of our lands by the government, its agencies or representatives, companies or individual speculators will be tolerated forthwith.

2. That the Ikwerre people will employ all legitimate and democratic instruments at our disposal to resist any such forceful acquisition of our lands and resources, now or in the future.

3. We firmly demand the payment of reparation for all our seized and stolen lands from both the Nigerian and Rivers State Governments.

Realising the fact that our people are marginalised in all institutions, resulting from an official and deliberate conspiracy, we demand effective and adequate representation in all institutions in Nigeria, and hereby resolve that we shall within the confines of our constitutional and democratic rights, resist any further act(s) of policy that portend to marginalise our people in the present Rivers State and the larger Nigerian Federation. Cognisant of the fact that our right to self-determination, resource ownership and control cannot be actualised without the abolition of all anti-people laws and policies, we demand the immediate abolition of the following laws: The Land Use Act (as amended) in 1978; The Petroleum Act (as amended) in 1969, etc. These objectionable laws are repressive and cannot guarantee our survival if they continue to exist in our statute books; because they deny us the use of our God-given resources.

Aware of our vulnerability and susceptibility to political and other forms of manipulations by our age-long oppressors and exploiters, it is resolved hereby and we appeal to the International Community, the Economic community of West Africa States (ECOWAS), Organisation of African Unity (OAU), Commonwealth of Nations, the European Union (EU), the United Nations Organisation (UNO) and several other institutions and individuals concerned with human and environmental rights and indigenous and minority peoples' rights, to support and come to our aid in our just crusade for democratic rights, justice, equity and fair play.

Aware that the renaming of Rebisi to what is called Port Harcourt in 1913 is a violation of our right to self-determination and forceful deprivation of our ancestral ethnic identity, and an attempt to force the Ikwerre ethnic nationality into extinction, we demand that Port Harcourt should revert to its original name of OBOMOTU-REBISI forthwith. Aware that we have the right to self-determination and development as a distinct and homogenous people, we demand the immediate creation of an IKWERRE STATE (presently comprising Port Harcourt, Obio/Akpor, Ikwerre and Emohua Local Government Areas), as it remains one of the only viable means through which our wishes, aspirations and survival can be guaranteed since most parts of the current Rivers State do not want us. We resolve as a people to defend these declarations by every legal and democratic means possible in seeking the implementation of our demands. As a result, we will categorically employ all legal and democratic means at our disposal to achieve our objectives. We are ready and willing to meet and dialogue with representatives of the Nigerian government at the earliest practicable date to address these issues.

We express our solidarity with all oppressed peoples in Nigeria in their just struggle for justice and equity, particularly the Ogoni, the Ijaw, the Ogba, the Etche, the Efik, the Ibibio, the Ekid, the Ekpeye, the Igbo, the Urhobo, the Itsekiri, the Isoko, etc.

Finally, IYC is a democratic and non-violent body, committed to the promotion of peace and justice. We will adopt a policy of non-violent resistance in pursuit of the above legitimate aspirations. We believe in and are ready and willing to dialogue with any body or institution as a means of addressing and finding possible solutions to the various problems confronting the Ikwerre people. Ikwerre land bears our ancestral blood; it must bear our will now and in the future. The youths of Ikwerre ethnic nationality are irrevocably committed to the total emancipation of Ikwerre land from modernised slavery. It is time to say No! No to oppression. No to exploitation. No to marginalistion. No to alienation from our ancestral land. No! No! No! To everything that compromises our humanity and dignity as a people both in the Niger Delta and the Nigerian Federation.

The Oron Bill of Rights, 1999

The negative impacts of oil on the people of Oron in the Niger Delta are astonishing. Oil means poverty since peoples rights have been severely assaulted by the ecologically unfriendly practices of Oil Transnational Corporations

(TNCs). In addition, state laws and policies, as they relate to petroleum resources, expropriate the indigenous peoples of their 'right' to their natural resources. Oil-based environmental degradation and ethnic-based political domination have combined to alienate the people from the use of their natural resources for their own development.

Oil exploration and production is associated with a number of activities that devastate the environment. Such devastations from oil spills kill fish and agricultural crops. It also reduces nutrient value of the soil. Gas flares diminish agricultural productivity. These informed the representatives of the Oron nation, comprising of Oron popular organisations, to resolve as follows:

- That the destiny of the Oron people must be seen in terms of the total security of the Oron geopolitical space which includes the people, the land, the culture and its future;

- That the processes and actions leading to the achievement of their development should not be compromised nor left to others;

- That the Oron nation is prepared to exist within the Nigerian State provided that: (a) All portions of Oron land and adjoining coastline areas be returned to the Oron nation for its management and control; (b) The Oron nation is treated as state within the Niger Delta region; (c) Oron nation, as an entity, independently cooperates with all people and other nationalities, soliciting for their assistance in securing and advancing her culture and protecting her heritage as a micro indigenous nationality;

- Every region should control its resources 100%, from which it will allocate funds for running the central government.

- The control and composition of all security organisations be decentralised.

THE ORON BILL OF RIGHTS

The Bill of Rights of the Oron People Unanimously Adopted and Proclaimed by the General and Representative Assembly of the Oron Indigenous Ethnic Linguistic Nationality, Nigeria, at the Oron Civic Centre, Oron, Friday, 25th of June, 1999.

Under the Leadership and Guidance of Oron National Forum (ONAF), Oron Development Union (ODU), Oron Women Action Group (OWAG), Oron Youth Movement (OYOM), Oron Public Relations Committee (OPRC), Organised by ORON NATIONAL FORUM (ONAF) 200 Oron Road, Oron. 25 June, 1999

ENABLING RESOLUTION

We the proud youths and representatives of Oron people, conscious of our historical role as the custodians of posterity;

Aware of our duties as protectors of our people, culture, civilisation, heritage, destiny and rights as a free people and coherent nationality;

Fully informed about the status, experience and prospects of our people in the Nigerian society;

Do hereby at the Representative Conference in the Oron Metropolis on the 25th day of June, 1999 declare as follows:

- Whereas the Oron people comprising five Local Government Areas of Mbo, Udung-Uko, Okobo, Uruko Offong/Oruko and Oron in Akwa Ibom State of Nigeria had existed as an independent, sovereign nation for hundreds of years before the formation of Nigeria by the British imperial power;

- Whereas the Oron Nation and people were never in any way consulted before they, including their land, were compromised by the British into the Nigeria contraption;

- Whereas the Nigeria experience has completely manifested a threat that if not checked may culminate in the total extinction of the Oron people, land and culture.

Be it resolved and it is hereby resolved that in order to save the Oron Nation:

- Oron People, Youths and Women all over the world unite under their patriotic organisations; ONAF, OYOM, OPRC, OWAG and others to proclaim the ORON BILL OF RIGHT as the embodiment of the grievances, principles and line of action in irreversible commitment to Oron meaningful survival;

- That Oron youths, women and people support and/ or initiate any programme anywhere they deem fit for the achievement of the above purpose.

THE BILL OF RIGHTS OF THE ORON PEOPLE

All over the whole civilised world, the flame which provides warmth and beautifies every human society is said to be embedded in the youth who are also its herald of a new dawn and civilisation and to this end, we, the youths and people of Oron, drawn from 200 communities of the eleven traditional clans spread across the five Local Government Areas of Oron, Mbo, Udung-Uko, Uruko Offong/Oruko and Okobo of Oron Nation met today, the 25th day of June, 1999 at the civic centre, Oron to review the processes of our participation in the Nigerian State, a fate fostered on us by accident of history and respectively preview our match into the third millenium and accordingly state as follows:

1. That the Oron Nation had existed as a free sovereign and egalitarian society for hundreds of years before its coercive lumping into the amalgamated Nigeria in 1914 and is therefore older than Nigeria itself and should have been consulted before the exercise which signalled the beginning of the chastisements hitherto suffered by the Oron Nation.

2. That before the forcible incorporation of the Oron Nation into the Nigerian State in 1914, the land mass, territorial waters of Oron were larger than what has been arbitrarily determined for it today by the Nigerian State against what was identified in 1690s Dutch maps of old Calabar and Oron Intelligence Report in 1935.

3. That over the years, it has been widely established that the Oro people attach great importance to the creeks and water fronts, but frustratingly, they have continued to have the harrowing experience of having their waters and ocean fronts – their main source of sustenance gradually seized from them.

   The most conspicuous are:

i. The Stubs and Widenham creeks/forests, water fronts as well as Oron fishing ports dotted along the Atlantic, littoral forceful annexed by Eket division in 1974 through the instrumentality of a Military Governor of Eket extraction, late Jacob Udoakaha Esuene.

ii. That the Bakassi territorial area on the Oron eastern border, with the Cameroon Republic, was awarded in 1996 by the Federal Military Government to Cross River State in honour of some highly placed sons and daughters of that state for their closeness to Generals

Ibrahim Babangida and Sani Abacha against the position of informed representation, documented facts before and during the colonial/early post-independent era.

4. That the Oron people have never had their dream of belonging to a political configuration of their choice realised as evident in our memoranda to the Irikefe Panel on State Creation in 1975, the Political Bureau of 1986-87 and the 1996 Arthur Mbanefo Committee on States, Local Governments Creation and Boundary Adjustment thus showing organised efforts by the Nigerian State to systematically neutralise and annihilate Oro identity, culture and heritage from the face of the earth.

5. That occasioned by neglect, marginalisation, repression, discrimination and deprivations, the story of Oro participation in the contraption called Nigeria has been one of stagnation and underdevelopment.

   The following are examples:

i. No Oron man has ever been appointed or elected a governor of a state and from 1984 till date, none of our sons and daughters has been deemed fit to hold a ministerial position in spite of the fact that successive regimes in the country have zoned key positions to Akwa Ibom State.

ii. No known project has been undertaken by the state and federal governments within Oro during the period.

6. That although the Oron Nation has played host to oil exploration and exploitation activities which started with Shell in 1958 with capped wells dotted across the Oro landscape, there is nothing to show for it.

7. That despite the presence of Mobil Producing Nigeria Unlimited rigs within Oro territorial waters and in "disputed" waters, the Oron Nation has been

denied its due, following the abrogation of offshore - onshore dichotomy as representations for Oro Local Government Areas to be in core catchment area of Mobil Producing Nigeria Unlimited have continued to fall on deaf ears. Of specific note is the fact that even paltry compensations for the January 1998 oil spill have not been paid to most communities and individuals in the Oro speaking Local Government Areas.

8. That our environment has been seriously degraded and abused over the years following indiscriminate activities of oil companies. Most agonising is the continued pollution of our coastal waters, river creeks and streams through the dumping of poisonous substances in our deep ocean trenches. Without mincing words, such acts have nonetheless placed our ocean's abundant wealth in jeopardy causing gross impoverishment of many fisherfolk and disrupting lives of coastal habitats and fish nursery grounds. These acts have therefore become very frustrating since, right from the beginning, life in this part of Nigeria depends almost wholly on the sea. We live on the sea, die on the sea and as we come to see it today the prospects are dangerously grim and our hopes and security are dimming and worsening by the day. Oro people are encircled by the Nigerian State and its collaborators.

Now exploration activities have driven aquatic products from nearby fishing grounds into the high seas which requires expensive fishing gears such as large boats and out boat engines to enable our fishfolk to continue with their trade. But since then, these untold hardships caused us by the multinational oil companies and the Nigerian National Petroleum Company, NNPC no assistance has come from any quarter to cushion the effects of skyrocketing prices of fishing material.

9. That the unilateral determination and implementation of the Derivation Principle of Revenue Allocation by the Federal Government alone without inputs/representations from oil producing states and communities have been a major source of tension in the country. Such a policy has been left to the whims and caprices of the predatory military cliques who were until recently in control of power to the detriment of the oil producing areas.

10. That no positive impact of OMPADEC and Petroleum Trust Fund (PTF) services has been felt in Oro land since their inceptions despite contributions from resources harnessed from Oro land and waters.

11. That the decision of the federal government to address the developmental problems of the Niger Delta through the Niger Delta Development Commission, though laudable, is not all embracing as it grossly omits some oil producing communities of the Niger Delta and represents palpable acquiescence, until a marginalised community engages the government in fierce battles, it is apparently not disposed to accede to the people's demands.

12. We note with regret that the non-constitution of a governing council for Maritime Academy of Nigeria, Oro, has given the sole administrator of the institution the license to run the place like sole proprietorship. This has generated tension in our community. Most of the senior Oro personnel in the institution have been unjustly removed from service. Oro has been denied all benefits that should accrue to the community.

DECLARATION

In view of the above we, representatives of the Oron Nation, comprising Oron popular organisations, here gathered, to wit:

The Oron National Forum (ONAF), The Oron Development Union (ODU), The Oron Youth Movement (OYOM), The Oron Women's Action Group (OWAG), The Oron Revolutionary Youth Committee (ORAYCOM), The Oron Public Relations Committee (OPRC) and other popular, patriotic and democratic organisations, hereby declare as follows:

1. That the manifest destiny of the Oron Nation is in the hands of the Oron people, particularly the youth and broad masses.

2. That the achievement of the manifest destiny must be seen in the total security of the Oron geopolitical space which includes the people, the land, the culture and future.

3. That the processes and actions relevant in the achievement of the manifest destiny in no way be compromised by any Oron citizen even at the pains of death.

4. That the Oron Nation is prepared to exist within the Nigerian system if, and only if, the security of the land and people is assured by appropriate affirmative action by the Nigerian Sovereign State by way of a just, equitable and democratic conduct of the affairs of the Federal Republic of Nigeria through its constitutional, political administration and social policies nationwide and particularly as they affect the micro-minorities.

5. That the Oron Nation unequivocally rejects the 1999 Constitution of Nigeria on the following grounds:

a. That it is arbitrary and undemocratic, imposed by a military cabal committed only to sectionalist interests.

b. It woefully fails to address the special interest of the micro-nationalities in the country.

c. It does not respect and observe genuine federal principles upon which any viable pluralistic Nigerian political community must be built.

d. It has grave feudalistic elements meant to undermine the small ethnic nationalities and the management of their resources and development interests.

DEMANDS

Fully conscious of the above facts and their implications, the People of Oron demand the following:

1. All portions of Oron land and adjoining coasts, that is, (i) the territory between Oro and the Republic of Cameroon (now called Bakassi) which is part of Mbo Local Government in Oro and had since been managed under Okolo/Oron Country Council or Oron Local Government; (ii) Esuk Inwang in Okobo Local Government Area settled in favour of Okobo by a competent court of law; (iii) the Stubs and Widenham creek forests with the adjoining coastal waters be immediately returned to the Oron Nation.

2. The Oron Nation must be made a state within the Niger Delta Region.

3. That the Federal Republic of Nigeria be restructured in six regions among which is the Niger Delta Region, comprising Cross River, Akwa Ibom, Rivers, Bayelsa, Delta and Edo States. Each region logically will be made up of a group of states along geo-cultural lines.

4. The regions should form the federating units, each with the power to manage its affairs, particularly development, according to its cultural realities.

5. Every region should control its resources 100% from which it will allocate funds for running the central government.

6. The Central Government should only handle a small number of policies such as Foreign Affairs, Immigration, Currency, Customs, etc.

7. The control and composition of all security organisations be decentralised. For instance, the military should be controlled and formed on regional commands basis and administered as recommended by the Movement for National Reformation, Izon National Congress, Afenifere, Movement for the Survival of the Ogoni People (MOSOP), the Ohaneze, Uhrobo Union, The Alliance for Democracy, JACON and other patriotic, popular organisations in the country.

8. The convening of a Sovereign National Conference of Ethnic Nationalities is imperative and should be facilitated by the nationalities to draw up a true democratic, federal structure for Nigeria.

9. Oron people unequivocally and vigorously reject further existence in the present Akwa Ibom State owing to continuous marginalisation of Oron people by successive administrations all controlled by the majority Ibibio-Annang hegemony. This treatment has manifested in public appointments by the military controlled federal and state appointments as well as the Government of Governor Victor Attah.

10. Oron nation hereby authorizes its National Joint Committee on Plans and Strategy to take necessary steps towards working with Ibeno and Eastern Obolo (Andoni) ethnic nationalities for a concrete joint programme of self determination of the three peoples.

131

11.   Oro Nation solicits the cooperation of all peoples and the civilised world to come to her aid in securing and advancing her culture and protecting her heritage as a small indigenous nationality.

We, the Representatives of Oron People... hereby declare our total and everlasting commitment to the Bill of Rights of the Oron People as an article of faith. So help us God.

The Akalaka Declaration, 1999

On 10th January 1999, the Egi Ethnic Coalition met at Akalaka, their ancestral headquarters and deliberated on the total neglect and exploitation of the Egi Clan by both the federal /state government and oil companies. It also reflected sadly on the deliberate non-compliance by Elf with the 1993 Peace Agreement reached with Egi Clan, and declared as follows:

The Egi people demand, as a matter of right, complete control of their land and mineral resources, as well as their environment which has been subjected to serious degradation by the exploitation of Elf Oil Company.

The Egi people believe that their steady slide into extinction can only be reversed by self-determination. They are convinced that only a Sovereign National Conference can establish the basis for mutual peaceful co-existence of the various ethnic nationalities within Nigeria and of the continued existence of Nigeria as a corporate unit.

The Egi people condemn the human rights violence on the Egi people and on the people of the Niger Delta by the military dictatorship in conjunction with the oil companies. They are also committed to the promotion of inter and intra-ethnic harmony in the Niger Delta as the only means to achieve stability and sustainable development in the area.

The Warri Accord, 1999

This accord contains the resolutions reached between Warri families at the Warri National Conference held in Benin City. The accord provides that:

1. Urgent steps be taken to provide basic amenities such as constant electricity, potable water, good roads and dredging of riverine waterways with a view to achieving the rapid modernisation and urbanisation of riverine and township areas in Warri;

2. Vocational centres for training of skilled and semi-skilled crafts persons be established in order to alleviate poverty, thus encouraging self employment through fishing, farming, carpentry and other small scale cottage industries in the remote and riverine areas of Warri, particularly in host communities;

3. On their part, the Warri host communities, as owners of land and stakeholders in the development of the area, should raise and operate vibrant vigilantes to check, monitor, police and arrest any person caught vandalising pipelines and equipment.

First Niger Delta Indigenous Women's Conference, 1999

1. The National Youth Service Corps Decree of 1973 has been used to deny Niger Delta youths job opportunities in the region, particularly when they return from the mandatory one-year service in states outside the region;

2. There should be an immediate action plan for the development of states in the region, i.e. building of grade A roads and telecommunications networks,

tertiary institutions, hospitals, potable water, modern river transportation, etc.;

3. The demilitarisation of the Niger Delta and the immediate withdrawal of all military personnel from the region;

4. A review of tax laws in Nigeria to compel oil companies to pay their taxes to the state governments where they have their operational bases;

5. Greater responsibility for the devastation of the environment and more precise action to mitigate the economic and social consequences of the environmental degradation on the region. To this end, the conference called for:

    i.   The conduct of a thorough environmental audit of the Niger Delta;

    ii.   Negotiation with the communities through a bottom-up approach, on their development priorities;

    iii.   Oil companies operating in the region to carry out the Oloibiri Oil Museum Master Plan and pay damages for the environmental degradation of Oloibiri;

    iv.   Payment of a minimum of ₦10,000 bursary allowance annually to all Niger Delta students in tertiary institutions;

    v.   Special attention should be paid to the girl-child education.

The Niger Delta Peoples' Compact, 2008

A meeting facilitated by Action Aid Nigeria in 2008 with representatives from the nine (9) states that make up the

Niger Delta region and key opinion leaders, came up with what they called the Niger Delta Peoples' Compact. This compact consists of a set of demands focusing on the following issues:

- Security and the withdrawal of troops including rehabilitation of the militants (and a clear rejection of AFRICOM);
- Just and accountable grievance redress mechanisms;
- Rapid infrastructural development;
- Environmental protection;
- Social re-orientation for communities;
- Control of resources and fiscal federalism;
- Address the needs of persons with disabilities;
- Pass the Freedom of Information Bill (FOI); and
- Achieve increased focus on education, health, agriculture and youth employment.

12

SOME DEVELOPMENTAL POLICIES

There have been many attempts and many plans made in the past to improve the lives of the people of the Niger Delta Region of Nigeria. Sadly, each ended with very little to show for the time and resources spent. What follows in this chapter is from the report of **The Technical Committee on the Niger Delta.** This is not a classified document and our efforts here is to make this public document easily accessible. **The Technical Committee on the Niger Delta** was inaugurated in September 2008 and tasked by the then Vice President, Dr Goodluck Jonathan:[44]

I.   To collate, review and distil the various reports, suggestions and recommendations on the Niger Delta from the Willinks Commission Report (1958) to the present, and give a summary of the recommendations necessary for government action.

II. To appraise the summary recommendations and present a detailed short, medium and long term suggestion to the challenges in the Niger Delta.

III. To make and present to government any other recommendations that will help the Federal government achieve sustainable development, peace, human and environmental security in the Niger Delta region.

---

44   "Terms of Reference; The Technical Committee on the Niger Delta" September, 2008.

The Henry Willinks Commission

The first constitutional step taken to develop the Niger Delta Region was the Henry Willinks-led Minority Rights Commission in September 1957. The commission had the following terms of reference:

i. To ascertain the facts of the fears of the minorities in any part of Nigeria and to propose means of allaying those fears whether well or ill-founded;

ii. To advise on what safeguards should be included for this purpose in the Constitution of Nigeria;

iii. If, but only if, no other solution seems to the commission to meet the case, then as a last resort, to make detailed recommendations for the creation of one or more new states and in that case:

- To specify the precise area to be included in such state or states;

- To recommend the governmental and administrative structure most appropriate for it;

- To assess whether any state recommended would be viable from an economic and administrative point of view and what the effect of its creation would be on the region from which it would be created and on the federation;

iv. To report its findings and recommendations to the Secretary of State for the Colonies.

Upon his appointment, Sir Henry Willinks arrived and undertook a tour of the country and held public hearings all over the country over a period of 6 months. At the end, he made the following recommendations on the Niger Delta:

i. That the Niger Delta people have peculiar problems, which arose out of the difficulties of their terrain and therefore, the region should be regarded as a special area;

ii. That the development of the area needs special attention by government (Federal and the then Eastern government);

iii. That there should be a federal board appointed to direct the development of the area into channels, which would meet the peculiar problems of the people;

iv. That the board shall draw up special schemes to supplement existing schemes, which would be financed exclusively by the federal government with the cooperation of the regional governments;

v. There should be inserted in the concurrent list of the constitution of the country, a clause, development of special areas, to enable the federal government to gazette, from time to time, areas designated as special areas and make special plans for their development in collaboration with the regional (now states) governments;

vi. The special area designation shall not be abandoned until when provision for development had gone far enough;

vii. The declaration as a special area should serve as an opportunity for the people to put forward a plan of their own for their improvement;

viii. All nominations by government from the Niger Delta area should include people who are likely to criticise it;

ix. That the minorities should not be neglected so badly or oppressed that it rebels so that the federal government would be asked to send in troops to quell such rebellion;

x. That the federal government should declare as minority areas:

a. The areas of Calabar
b. The area of Edo speaking people.

Some of these recommendations were later included in the constitution which later saw the establishment of the Niger Delta Development Board (NDDB).

The Niger Delta Development Board

In 1961, Nigeria's federal parliament enacted the Niger Delta Development Board Act of 1961 to comply with Section 14 of the 1960 Constitution. Section 14 of the 1960 Constitution established the Niger Delta Development Board to provide physical development for the Niger Delta region. The section enjoins

1. There shall be for the Niger Delta, a Board which shall be styled the Niger Delta Development Board.

2. The members of the Niger Delta Development Board shall be -

   a. A person appointed by the Governor-General of the Federation of Nigeria who shall be chairman;

   b. A person appointed by the Governor of Western Nigeria;

   c. A person appointed by the Governor of Eastern Nigeria; and

   d. Such other persons as may be appointed in such manner as may be prescribed by the parliament of the Federation of Nigeria to represent the inhabitants of the Niger Delta.

3. A member of the Niger Delta Development Board shall vacate his office in such circumstance as may be prescribed by the Parliament of the Federation of Nigeria.

4. The Niger Delta Development Board shall be responsible for advising the government of the Federation of Nigeria and the government of Western Nigeria and Eastern Nigeria with respect to the physical development of the Niger Delta, and in order to discharge that responsibility the Board shall -

    a. Cause the Niger Delta to be surveyed in order to ascertain what measures are required to promote its physical development;

    b. Prepare schemes designed to promote the physical development of the Niger Delta together with estimates of the costs of putting such schemes into effects;

    c. Submit to the government of the Federation and the government of Western Nigeria and Eastern Nigeria an initial report describing the survey of the Niger Delta and the measures that appear to the Board to be desirable in order to promote the physical development thereof, having regard to the information derived from the survey, and subsequent annual reports describing the work of the Board and the measures taken in pursuance of its advice.

5. The Parliament of the Federation of Nigeria may make such provision as may appear to be necessary or desirable for enabling the Niger Delta Development Board to discharge its functions under this section.

    The board, however, could not provide any meaningful development for the Niger Delta Region because of lack of political will and commitment.

The 1963 Constitution

After three years of independence, Nigeria gave itself a brand new constitution. The Constitution of the Federal Republic of Nigeria (1963) was the first constitution fashioned out for the country by its own people. Under that constitution, the principle of derivation for minerals extracted was clearly entrenched as follows:

i. By virtue of Section 140(1), the federal government pays to each region 50% of the royalty or mining rent in respect of any proceed got from each region in respect of mineral exploited in each region.

ii. The federal government then makes available 30% of the amount received in respect of all royalties and rents to the distributable pool for sharing amongst the three regions.

iii. By virtue of Section 140(5) of the 1963 constitution, "minerals" includes mineral oil.

Even though crude oil had been discovered in the country earlier, in 1956, the constitution did not discriminate between any kinds of minerals. In spite of the 50% derivation principle enshrined, the constitution also went a step further to give a special recognition to the Niger Delta as an area needing special attention.

A special chapter, Chapter 12 (Miscellaneous) was inserted in the constitution, which made provisions for the Niger Delta. This chapter outlined various measures for the region as follows:

i. Under Section 159, the constitution created a special board known as the Niger Delta Development Board (NDDB) with membership which included, as prescribed by parliament, such persons that represent the inhabitants of the Niger Delta;

142

ii. The board was to advise the FG and the Eastern and Western regional governments on the physical development of the Niger Delta;

iii. The board was to cause the Niger Delta to be surveyed to ascertain the measures required to promote its physical development;

iv. Prepare schemes, complete with estimates, for the physical development of the Niger Delta.

For the purpose of expediency and the execution of the Biafran Civil War, the section of the constitution relating to revenue was abrogated by the military government.

Isaac Dina Commission of Inquiry

A commission of inquiry under Chief Isaac Dina was set up in 1967 during the early years of the civil war. The mandate was to review the system of revenue allocation in the federation. According to Tom Forrest:

> ...the result of this commission was never published, but most of the ideas in the report were later adopted. The report recommended greater financial responsibilities for the Federal Government in the areas of higher education, roads, health and industry. There was to be an enlarged Distributable Pool Account at the center through which the states shared their revenues and a downgrading of the derivation principle in revenue allocation, which it was argued, had accentuated uneven development and regional conflict in the past.[45]

According to Henry Bienen, the downgrading of the derivation policy is suspect for the following reason:

> The governments of the Northern and Western Regions had favoured the principle of derivation prior to 1960 when groundnuts and cocoa were the major sources of export revenue. But when petroleum was found in the east and

---

45   T. FORREST, *Politics and Economic Development in Nigeria,* (Colorado, West Press, Inc; 1993), 49.

delta ... the Northern and Western regions reversed their arguments and became the proponent of derivation as a major component of a revenue allocation formula.[46]

The Belgore Report, 1992

In 1992, a Judicial Commission of Inquiry headed by Hon. Justice Alfa Belgore, then Justice of the Supreme Court, was set up to look into the causes of fuel shortages in Nigeria. One of the terms of reference for the commission was to identify the root causes of continual communal dissatisfaction and violence in the oil-producing areas and to suggest ways of improving upon the measures so far taken by government in that regard. The commission concluded that the root cause of the problems of the Niger Delta was **neglect**. The commission recommended, amongst other things, that:

i. A thirty-year development plan should be prepared for the systematic development of the oil-producing communities;

ii. East-West road which traverses the major oil producing states be dualised and improved;

iii. East-West rail line be constructed from Calabar to Lagos and to link the line to an improved national rail network.

OMPADEC 1992-2000

Oil Minerals Producing Areas Development Commission (OMPADEC 1992-2000) was established by the military government of General Ibrahim Babangida under Decree No 23 of 1992. The purpose and mandate to the commission was to address the years of neglect of the Niger Delta region.

---

46   H. BIENEN, "Oil Revenues And Policy Choice In Nigeria", World Bank Staff Working Papers #592, Washington DC, 1983, 3.

Section 2 of Decree No 23 states that the objectives of the commission shall be:

i. Receive and administer the monthly sums from the allocation of the Federation Account in accordance with confirmed ratio of oil production in each state for the rehabilitation and development of all mineral producing areas, so as to tackle the ecological problems that have arisen from the exploration of oil minerals;

ii. Determine and identify, through the commission and the respective oil mineral-producing states, the actual oil mineral-producing areas and embark on the development of projects properly agreed upon with the local communities of the oil mineral-producing areas;

iii. Consult with the relevant federal and state government authorities on the control and effective methods of tackling the problems of oil pollution and spillages;

iv. Liaise with the various oil companies on matters of pollution control;

v. Obtain from the Nigerian National Petroleum Corporation the proper formula for actual oil mineral production of each state, local government area and distribution of projects, services and employment of personnel in accordance with recognised percentage production;

vi. Consult with the federal government through the presidency, the state, local governments and oil mineral–producing communities regarding projects, services and all other requirements relating to the special fund (derivation revenue);

vii. Render annual returns to the President, Commander-in-Chief of the Armed Forces and copy the state and local governments on all matters relating to the special fund;

viii. Advice the federal, state and local governments on all matters relating to the special fund;

ix. Liaise with the oil-producing companies regarding the proper number, location and other relevant data regarding oil mineral-producing areas; and

x. Execute other works and perform such other functions which in the opinion of the Commission, is geared towards the development of the oil mineral-producing areas.

Section 4a(2) of the Allocation of Revenue (Federation Account) (Amendment Act No 106 of 1992) provided that, three per cent (3%) of the federation account derived from mineral revenue be paid to the commission and shall be used for the rehabilitation and development of the oil mineral-producing areas on the basis of the ratio of the oil produced in the particular areas, and not on the basis of dichotomy of on-shore or off-shore oil production. Like its predecessors, OMPADEC consequently failed to promote the development of the Niger Delta region.

The Etiebet Report, 1994

In November 1993, the Federal Government set up an Inter-Ministerial Fact-Finding team, headed by Chief Don Etiebet (then Minister of Petroleum), with Chiefs Melford Okilo (then Minister of Commerce & Tourism) and Alex Ibru (then Minister of Internal Affairs) and officials of the petroleum industry: Group Managing Director (GMD), Nigeria National Petroleum Corporation (NNPC); Group Executive Director (GED), National Petroleum Investment Management Services (NAPIMS); Director of Petroleum

Resources; Chairman, Oil Mineral Producing Areas Development Commission (OMPADEC); Chief Executive Officers (CEOs) of all oil companies, etc. as members.

The team carried out a comprehensive tour of the oil-producing communities in the country to ascertain the causes of their grievances; assessed the level of development on ground and made recommendations to government. In its report, the team stated as follows:

1. Most of the communities lack basic necessities of life;
2. Basic facilities like roads, potable water, electricity, health care, and education are completely absent in many communities and not functioning in others where they exist;
3. These basic amenities and more modern facilities were available in the estates or platforms where oil workers live sometimes within the same or nearby communities. The demonstration effects of the robust lifestyle of these workers in contrast to the wretched living conditions and hopelessness of the communities is such that evokes hostility and strong feelings of deprivation and injustice within communities;
4. The degradation of the environment has destroyed farmlands and aquatic life and affected the economic life of all;
5. Marine erosion has seriously threatened the land area in the riverine communities adjoining off-shore oil fields in the different states. At several points, the land is being washed away at a disturbing level annually;
6. Widespread gas flaring has inflicted untold hardships on human, plant and animal life. For instance, agricultural production is drastically reduced as increased atmospheric temperature kills plants within the vicinity of the flares;

7. The quality of social amenities provided, if at all, to communities by oil companies are below the standards provided elsewhere in the world by the same oil companies. For instance, roads constructed in oil-producing communities are usually not accessible all seasons of the year. Furthermore, there are narrow and dangerous bridges, no drainage, and existing roads rendered impassable by heavy equipment belonging to the oil companies or by floods;

8. Unemployment among the youths is high dangerously;

9. The communities generally lack telecommunication facilities, and are therefore out of touch with events outside their locations;

10. Location of oil facilities in competing communities have heightened long-standing inter-communal conflicts resulting in extensive destruction of entire villages, schools and other facilities;

11. There was a high incidence of pollution caused by oil spillages, leakages, and other discharges into the environment. And the oil companies have not taken action in line with international environmental standards to control and ameliorate the environmental impacts of their operations, and the extent of impact on the communities have also not been systematically evaluated and documented;

12. On the whole, the scale of physical neglect of the oil-producing areas is enormous.

The following recommendations were made and classified into immediate, medium and long-term solutions:

i.   The Belgore Commission of Inquiry Report relating to the Niger Delta should be implemented;

ii. Compensation should be paid immediately for settlement of people displaced as a result of communal clashes resulting from disputes relating to oil exploration;

iii. Immediate re-organisation of OMPADEC to decentralise its operational structure;

iv. Generators should be provided to small island communities for immediate provision of electricity pending the provision of electricity through gas turbines using flared gas;

v.   Borehole water should immediately be provided in the communities with the greatest need;

vi. The Yenagoa-Kolo-Nembe-Brass Road should be constructed with a road leading to Abua and Oloibiri towns respectively;

vii. Petroleum products distribution stations and facilities should be established in the communities;

viii. Basic health and education facilities, including supply of equipment, drugs, vaccines, and blood banks, and even personnel should be provided in communities;

ix. Ongoing rates of compensation for loss of land and economic trees should be published with a view to having an up-to-date rate book to avoid arbitrariness in compensation payment by oil companies;

x.   There should be sustained development of infrastructure and social amenities, including housing and cottage industries in communities and their environs;

xi.   Small holder agricultural and fisheries concerns should be organised, and agriculture and fishery cooperatives should be promoted in catchment areas;

xii. Roads should be constructed to link the remote communities with their neighbours and to reduce the long and tedious detours of travelling by boat to get to adjoining communities;

xiii. A comprehensive master plan for the coordination of development of the oil-producing areas should be commissioned;

xiv. There should be review of: (a) The Mineral Act; (b) The Petroleum Act; (c). The Oil Pipeline Act; and (d) related legislation in order to provide through statutes, legal provisions that promote harmonious relationships and the development of the oil industry for the benefit of the economy, the oil companies and host communities;

xv.   Dredging and expanding of canals and construction of embankment and jetties in the riverine communities should be carried out;

xvi. An all-seasons concrete dual carriage way complete with drainage and electricity to link the coastal states as well as other major cities and towns should be constructed;

xvii. Gas flare should be reduced by design and construction of plants to harness associate gas for supply to industries;

xviii. Specialised oil and gas Export Processing Zones (EPZs) should be established in the three main oil-producing states to stimulate industrial development and growth in the communities;

xix. The following revenues should be allocated to the development of oil-producing communities; (a) 5% of total production (net of production cost) (b) 2% of total annual budget of the oil companies, to be managed by a consortium of the oil companies, OMPADEC, NNPC, etc; (c) At least 5% total oil revenue for the rehabilitation of the oil-producing areas environment;

xx. A comprehensive study of coastal areas should be undertaken to address the problems of erosion which has displaced many people living in coastal communities, with a view to protecting or relocating them;

xxi. Oil companies should conserve and protect the environment, and should ensure minimal discharge into the environment;

xxii. Each company should prepare and submit to the appropriate authority, a medium to long-term environment outline for containing waste and clearing up emissions in a safe manner using international standards. The rehabilitation of the already-degraded environment which is lawfully the responsibility of the polluter should be enforced;

xxiii. Decree No. 86 of 1992 should be strictly and faithfully enforced and complied with, especially enforcing Environmental Impact Assessments(EIAs);

xxiv. An in-depth study should be carried out to identify the pollution load in each area and also characterise the level of degradation suffered by communities affected by pollution;

xxv. A study of the socio-economic and health impact on communities should be undertaken;

xxvi. Environmental auditing of ongoing oil operations should be undertaken;

xxvii. An environmental pollution-monitoring programme should be mandatory in all oil-producing communities.

The Vision 2010 Report, 1996

On September 27, 1996, General Sani Abacha inaugurated the Vision 2010 Committee to produce a blueprint for the development of the country. Chaired by Chief (Dr.) E. A. O. Shonekan, the committee was made of 247 selected Nigerians. The terms of reference of the committee included:

- To constructively analyse why Nigeria's development has not progressed in relation to its potentials, 36years after independence;

- To envision where Nigeria would want to be in 50 years after independence; and

- To draw up a blueprint and action plan for translating this shared vision into reality.

Although this report did not make a specific recommendation in relation to the Niger Delta, nevertheless, it made one of the most profound and far-reaching recommendations with respect to the proper and efficient operations of the oil industry. The report posited that in order for the country to attain its vision of development by the year 2010, it has to fully develop the oil and gas sector to provide the launch pad for developing the rest of the economy, and developing a sustainable international competitive edge.

The report affirmed that Nigeria's 28% contribution to the total global gas flare was a source of ecosystem destabilisation, heat stress, and acid precipitation which has induced the destruction of freshwater fishes and forest in the coastal areas of the country. The committee, therefore, recommended that in order to achieve a safe and healthy environment that secures the economic and social well-being of the present and future generations, incidents of oil spillages, gas flaring and oil pollution should be eliminated.

Report of the UN Special Rapporteur on Human Rights Situation in Nigeria (1997)

The UN in 1997 appointed a special rapporteur on Nigeria to undertake a review of the country's human rights' situation and report to the world body. The special rapporteur visited the Niger Delta, especially Ogoni. In his report to the UN, the special rapporteur observed and expressed concerns about the human rights situation in Nigeria, particularly the situation in the Niger Delta, and made the following specific recommendations on the region:

i.   An independent agency should be established in consultation with Shell Petroleum Development Company (SPDC), Movement for the Survival of Ogoni People (MOSOP) and other groups for the purpose of determining all issues relating to environmental damage due to oil exploration and other operation; furthermore, issues of environmental protection in Ogoni and the entire Niger Delta including the findings of the rapporteur should be made public;

ii.   The oil companies' security personnel wearing the same uniform as that of the Nigeria Police should be discontinued;

iii. The oil companies, including SPDC, should initiate more development projects in consultation with the communities concerned;

iv. An independent judicial mechanism with the mandate of ensuring early disposal of compensation claims should be established;

v. Greater attention should be paid to and more resources deployed for the protection and promotion of the economic and social rights of the region's people, especially in the area of health, shelter and education;

vi. There should be increased budgetary funding of the health sector. The government should aid health institutions to procure modern medical equipment.

vii. Effective disease prevention and management strategies should be initiated and the population properly educated about diseases such as AIDS;

viii. Prompt compensation should be paid to persons whose human rights have been violated;

ix. The federal and state governments should adopt effective policies, measures and programmes aimed at increasing housing and access to housing in Nigeria, especially through the provision of mortgage financing and the development of primary mortgage institutions;

x. The government should ratify the Convention against Torture and Other Cruel, Inhuman or Degrading Treatment or Punishment.

The Popoola Report, 1998

After the death of General Sani Abacha, General Abdulsalami Abubakar at the instance of the federal government convened a 22-member Presidential Committee on Development Options for the Niger Delta. The committee was headed by the then General Officer Commanding 82 Division, Major General Oladayo Popoola. All the military administrators of the oil-producing states were members, as well as the Honourable Ministers of Works and Housing, Education, Water Resources, Health, Power and Steel including representatives of Oil Mineral Producing Areas Development Commission (OMPADEC), Secretary to Government of the Federation, Project Implementation and Monitoring Committee (PIMCO), and Principal Staff Officer to Commander-in-Chief, among others.

The terms of reference of the committee were as follows:

1. To study the proposals by Programme Implementation and Monitoring Committee (PIMCO) on the sustainable development of the Niger Delta;

2. To ascertain the projects undertaken in relation to education, electricity, water supply, roads and canal construction and the rehabilitation of health care and other facilities;

3. To verify current projects being undertaken by Oil Mineral Producing Areas Development Commission (OMPADEC) and Petroleum Trust Fund, as well as the oil companies, other governmental agencies and non-governmental organisations.

4. To make appropriate recommendations relating to what can be done before and at the end of the Abubakar administration.

During a period of 22 days, the committee undertook a tour of the Niger Delta, received and reviewed memoranda from the public and special interest groups including state governments, the oil companies and NGOs, and engaged in direct interaction with major stakeholders in the region, especially the oil companies, the state governments, opinion leaders, etc., and came out with its findings. In its report to the Commander-in-Chief, General Abdulsalam Abubakar, the committee noted that:

1.   The Niger Delta deserves the nation's attention, not merely as a result of the oil it produces but because it is a component of Nigeria, and therefore crucial for the nation to find enduring solutions to the problems of the area;

2.   The problem of underdevelopment in the Niger Delta is a long-standing issue even before the advent of oil, which successive governments have attempted unsuccessfully to tackle and this has been largely due to administrative failures.

3.   The presence of small, isolated and mutually distrustful communities in the region has over the years become a source of major constraint to the overall development of the region.

4.   Even though enormous resources have been pumped into the region, its development has hardly improved due to lack of an all-encompassing initiative that lays the foundation for the process of development.

5.   Efforts of past administrations to address the problems of the region have been inadequate in terms of funding and poor implementation;

6.   The geographical terrain of the Niger Delta makes the provision of infrastructure difficult and expensive, the creeks and rivers make transportation and communication a nightmare, and much of the mangrove swamp forest constitutes natural habitat for diseases;

7.   There is the growing emergence of an underclass population in the Niger Delta, composed mostly of youths that are poor, ill-educated and prone to criminal behaviours;

8.   Criminal activities have become mixed with genuine community agitations or protest and even if community agitations were addressed, criminal tendencies are likely to continue;

9.   Of all the Niger Delta states, Bayelsa has the greatest need for infrastructure for rapid and meaningful socio-economic development;

10.   There are too many statutes in the oil industry and there is a need to consolidate all the statutes so as to reduce regulatory burdens and overcome competing legal and inhibiting requirements.

The committee therefore made far-reaching recommendations to the federal government as a way of addressing the problems of underdevelopment, unrest and insecurity in the region. It recommended as follows:

1.   A committee of experts should be set up to review and consolidate existing mineral and oil-related statutes with a view to (a) Ensuring prompt payment of compensation to host communities by oil companies through compulsory arbitration proceedings; (b) Sustaining good environmental standards in host

communities; (c) Creating and enforcing corporate responsibility by oil companies in host communities, (d) Creating new oil-related offences and upward review of existing punishment for offences; and (e) Promoting the prosecution of all forms of rights violations arising from oil operations and ensuring that corporate practice conforms with international laws and requirements;

2. Purchase of boats for the states of the Niger Delta which will be used in the same way as buses which were purchased for mass transit on land for other states;

3. Establish through private sector participation petrol stations in five oil-producing communities with relatively high population;

4. Increase the level of federal presence in Bayelsa State;

5. Build two technical colleges and site one each in Bayelsa and Delta States;

6. The rural electrification projects of the Federal Ministry of Power & Steel which require about ₦1.725 billion to be completed should be funded before May 29, 1999;

7. NEPA should take over and repair the gas turbine plant supplying electricity to Yenagoa;

8. The federal government should offer additional incentives to entrepreneurs to encourage the establishment of industries in the Niger Delta;

9. More schools should be renovated in oil-producing areas as part of short-term remedial measures;

10. In their dealings with oil companies, communities should accept facilities which contribute to development rather than cash;

11. Oil companies should ensure that junior and unskilled labour are recruited from the communities in which they operate;

12. Mobile boats acting as clinics should be provided as an interim strategy for addressing the health situation in most riverine areas of the Niger Delta;

13. Electricity from the Kolo creek gas turbine in Bayelsa State should be extended to neighbouring towns and villages in the area;

14. Government should initiate action leading to the production of a 20-year regional master plan for the Niger Delta by setting up a Coordinating Committee for the Niger Delta Master Plan (CCND).

In conclusion, the committee suggested some projects to be implemented in the Niger Delta states, and classified them into short, medium and long-term projects. The report of this committee was concluded and submitted on 15th March, 1999 but its recommendations were not acted upon before the handing over of government to civil rule on May 29, 1999

Niger-Delta Development Commission (NDDC, 2000-2008)

In 2000, President Olusegun Obasanjo submitted to the National Assembly a Bill for an Act to provide for the repeal of the Oil Mineral Producing Areas Development Commission Decree 23 of 1992. Among other things, the President's goal was to establish a new commission with a reorganised management and administrative structure for more effective use of the special funds it will receive from the federation account to tackle ecological and other related problems arising from the exploration of oil minerals in the Niger Delta areas. The Niger Delta Development Commission (NDDC) Act was subsequently passed into law in 2000, and that established the commission. Section 7 of the Act 2000 provides that the commission shall:

i.   Formulate policies and guidelines for the development of the Niger Delta area:

ii.   Conceive, plan and implement (in accordance with set rules and regulations) projects and programmes for sustainable transformation of the areas including roads, jetties and waterways, health, education, employment, industrialisation, agriculture and fisheries, housing and urban development, water supply, electricity and telecommunication;

iii.   Cause the Niger Delta area to be surveyed in order to ascertain measures which are necessary to promote its physical and socio-economic developments;

iv.   Prepare master plans and schemes designed to promote the physical development of the Niger Delta area and the estimates of the costs of implementing such master plans and schemes;

v.   Implement all the measures approved for the development of the Niger Delta area by the federal government and the member-states of the commission;

vi.   Identify factors inhibiting the development of the Niger Delta area and assist the member-states in the formulation and implementation of policies to ensure sound and efficient management of the resources of the Niger Delta;

vii.   Assess and report on any project funded and carried out in the Niger Delta area by oil and gas producing companies or any other company including non-governmental organisations, and ensure that funds released for such projects are properly utilised to tackle ecological and environmental problems that arose from exploration of oil mineral in the Niger Delta area and advise the federal government and member-states on the prevention and control of oil spillages, gas flaring and environmental pollutions;

viii. Liaise with the various oil mineral and gas prospecting and producing companies on all matters of pollution prevention and control; and

ix. Execute such other works and perform such other functions which, in the opinion of the commission, are required for the sustainable development of the Niger Delta area and its people.

Special Security Committee: The Ogomudia Report, 2001

The Special Security Committee on Oil Producing Areas was headed by the then Chief of Army Staff, Lieutenant-General Alexander Odeareduo Ogomudia. It was set up by the federal government to address the prevailing situation in the oil-producing areas when there was an unprecedented vandalisation of oil pipelines, disruptions, kidnappings, extortions and a general state of insecurity, especially in the oil and gas industry. The committee made the following recommendations:

1. That adequate measures should be taken to secure the oil-producing areas: in particular, the operational facilities and equipment of the Nigerian Armed Forces and the Nigeria Police, especially the Nigerian Navy, should be modernised with offshore patrol vessels to enable them patrol the Exclusive Economic Zone (EEZ);

2. All oil pipelines should be maintained to meet international standards in order to prevent ruptures and its consequential damage to the environment;

3. Security of oil pipelines should be community based;

4. The use of military force in resolving restiveness should be discouraged;

5. Instead of the 13% derivation, which is hardly adequate, the derivation principle should be increased to a minimum of 50%;

6. The dichotomy between onshore/offshore oil exploration activities should be removed to allow for sustained peace in the oil-producing states;

7. The Niger Delta Development Commission (NDDC) should be adequately funded and the indigenes should be made to participate fully and meaningfully in development projects designed for them;

8. The Federal Government of Nigeria should immediately commence construction of the Lagos-Calabar coastal road passing through Ogun, Ondo, Edo, Delta, Bayelsa, Rivers, and Akwa Ibom States with linkages to Imo, Abia, Forcados, Burutu, Nembe, Brass, Bonny and Bakassi;

9. There should be an established Mass Coastal/ Marine Transportation System for the oil-producing communities;

10. The various governments (federal, state and local), should take up the responsibility of developing the oil-producing communities, instead of the oil companies;

11. Government should fully pay the 13% derivation stipulated in the constitution;

12. The payment of compensation due to oil spillages should be appropriately worked out and addressed;

13. The state governments should set up identifiable and transparent programmes for the utilisation of the 13% derivation funds, which should target the oil-producing communities;

14. Conscious efforts should be taken to adequately ensure the employment of persons from oil-producing communities in oil companies and the Nigerian National Petroleum Corporation (NNPC);

15. Agriculture and agro-based industries should be established in the oil-producing communities to further create employment in the area;

16. A technical team should be set up to explore ways to see to the development of Niger Delta beaches into tourism spots;

17. Several vocational/skill acquisition programmes should be established for the oil-producing communities;

18. There should be programmes for gifted students from oil-producing areas to attract them into the employment of oil companies and progressively enable them to work up towards top level management;

19. Governments at the federal, state, local levels and Niger Delta Development Commission (NDDC) should establish new towns and settlements through reclamation of swamp land.

20. The federal government should be primarily responsible for the development of the oil-producing areas by developing interstate roads, rail lines, hospitals and education centres;

21. Oil companies, including refineries, should supply electricity and water to communities within 5km radius of their facilities;

22. States should embark on the construction of feeder roads and provision of educational facilities and equipment;

23. Government should compel oil companies to fully comply with environmental regulations relating to their operations;

24. State governments should set up development agencies where a certain percentage of the derivation funds shall be channelled;

25. Oil companies should observe international rules and regulations as they relate to their operations within communities;

26. The oil companies should adhere to memoranda of understanding signed by them and should contribute to the provision of social amenities and development of their areas of operations;

27. There should be consultation and cooperation within communities and a well-articulated information strategy for spreading positive messages of peace in the Niger Delta;

28. Oil companies should deliberately award contracts to contractors from oil-producing communities as a way of empowering local people;

29. The government should immediately review the following existing laws which are sources of contention within the region: (a) Oil Pipeline Act, 1959; (b) Oil Terminal Dues Act, 1965; (c) Petroleum Act, 1969; (d) Land Use Act, 1978; (e) Associated Gas Re-Injection Act, 1979; (f.) Land (Title Vesting)Act, 1993;

30. The government should embark on massive erosion control, shore protection and reinforcement;

31. There should be payment of compensation to communities impacted by oil spillages, where such spillages are not acts of sabotage, and in the case of sabotage, third parties impacted by oil spill should be compensated;

32. Nigerian National Petroleum Corporation (NNPC), Department of Petroleum Resources (DPR) and the oil companies should take appropriate steps to treat waste from oil companies so that it meets international standards of safety before it is discharged into the environment;

33. All gas flaring should be terminated in 2008 with no further deadline extension.

White Paper Report of the Presidential Panel on National Security, 2003

When the security breaches and inter-communal disturbances persisted, the federal government at the instance of President Olusegun Obasanjo set up a Presidential Panel on National Security to explore strategies for achieving high levels of security of life and property.

The panel observed that:

1. Insecurity in the region is a long-standing problem, which has been expressed since the First Republic in form of agitations and petitions. It has, however, grown in intensity in recent times because of neglect.

2. The region's restiveness is an expression by host-communities of opposition to what they perceive as the destruction of their means of livelihood and their eco-system by oil exploration/exploitation without adequate arrangement to mitigate the prevailing hardships arising therefrom;

3. The communities, through their youth and, in recent times, their women, confront the oil companies through various means of protest including seizure/vandalisation of oil installations and kidnapping of oil workers;

4. To address the restiveness, the oil companies have been paying some form of compensation to gravely polluted areas and have provided some social services on a voluntary basis and usually under pressure from communities;

5. The federal government, over the years, had set up the Niger Delta Development Board (NDDB), the Oil Mineral Producing Areas Development Commission (OMPADEC) and its successor, the Niger Delta Development Commission (NDDC) to tackle the development of the area. The impact of the first two was not felt, thereby, necessitating the establishment of the NDDC;

6. The current positive effort being made by the NDDC can best be consolidated through effective partnerships with the various levels of governments (federal, state and local) and the oil companies.

Flowing from these findings, the panel made a number of recommendations:

i. Oil companies should be made to maintain environmental standards comparable to the high environmental standards of their home countries.

ii. Government should insist through new legislation at appropriate levels that the polluter pays, which is a globally recognised norm.

iii. The existing National Youth Policy should be promptly and faithfully implemented by government so as to address key aspects of social and economic inadequacies that predispose youth in the region to violence and manipulation.

Report on First International Conference on Sustainable Development of the Niger Delta, NDDC and UNDP, 2003

This report recommends a new development paradigm to address the concerns of the Niger Delta. In a seven-point development, it proposes using the region's vast oil wealth to create an environment that allows people to flourish, live valued and dignified lives, overcome poverty, enjoy a peaceful atmosphere and sustain their environment. The agenda is a people-centred and sustainable framework requiring the involvement of all stakeholders, including local, state and federal governments, the NDDC, the oil companies and the entire private sector, civil society organisations, the people of the region and development partners.

1. **Agenda One –** *Promote peace as the foundation for development:* There cannot be any meaningful human development without peace. A peace agenda must include education, easier access to justice and a more equitable distribution of resources.

2. **Agenda Two –** *Make local governance effective and responsive to the needs of the people:* Governance is very central to achieving meaningful development outcomes. The effectiveness of governance, especially at the local government level, is an issue of serious concern. At the core of promoting effective governance is the urgent need to institutionalise the practices of accountability, transparency and integrity to guide the flow of development resources at all levels.

3. **Agenda Three –** *Improve and diversify the economy:* The Niger Delta region, with its stock of natural and human resources, offers immense opportunities for developing a diversified and growing economy. A diversified economy would reduce dependence on oil and gas, jumpstart new industries and provide sustainable livelihoods. A growth pole strategy would forge closer links between industries and the production of agricultural and mineral products, and galvanise local economies.

4. **Agenda Four –** *Promote social inclusion and improved access to social services:* A major concern is the region's longstanding exclusion from the mainstream of Nigeria's socioeconomic and political activities. The majority of the people in the delta live on the margins. Reducing exclusion and achieving more even-handed development will depend on the empowerment of socially marginalised groups and individuals, stronger social institutions and infrastructure, and the development of the capacity of existing local groups.

5. **Agenda Five –** *Promote environmental sustainability to preserve the means of people's sustainable livelihoods:* The mainstreaming of environmental sustainability into all development activities must be complemented by proactive steps to conserve natural resources; to reduce pollution, especially from oil spills and gas flares; and to set and achieve adequate targets for clean air and water and soil fertility. These should be backed by rigorous enforcement of environmental laws and standards.

6. **Agenda Six –** *Take an integrated approach to HIV&AIDS:* Strong advocacy from top policymakers

should be coupled with public awareness campaigns on the multidimensional nature of HIV & AIDS and public education on the laws against some risky traditional practices. State and local governments, the NDDC, oil companies, other private sector enterprises, NGOs and donors should collectively improve the quality and accessibility of health care and HIV&AIDS facilities and equipment, and institute actions to curb the epidemic.

7. **Agenda Seven** – *Build sustainable partnerships for the advancement of human development:* Many stakeholders must work together to achieve meaningful change. All levels of government and the NDDC, the oil companies, the organised private sector, civil society organisations and development agencies should form partnerships around plans for sustainable development and the attainment of the Millennium Development Goals (MDGs).

The Niger Delta Regional Development Master Plan, 2004

In the year 2000, the National Assembly passed a Bill for the establishment of a development commission for the Niger Delta Region, known as the Niger Delta Development Commission (NDDC). This commission, which was an intervention by President Olusegun Obasanjo, was directly under the supervision of the presidency. Part of the mandate of the commission as enshrined in the Act was to carry out a detailed study of the region with a view to providing a master plan for the wholistic development of the region. The master plan presents major development actions for intervention which would accelerate the development of the Niger Delta.

1. Physical Infrastructure

a. Provision of essential physical infrastructure such as reliable power supply, telecommunication, and transportation, which are essential for business and residency;

b. Provision of physical infrastructure in urban and rural areas and designation of some areas as growth communities which will enjoy priority projects;

c. Provision and improvement of existing telecommunication facilities in urban and rural areas to ensure interconnectivity amongst communities and their connection to the national telecommunication services. There is also a recommendation for the installation of a V-Sat which will provide internet and e-mail connectivity across the region;

d. Building and supply of reliable energy to all communities through the national grid or through extended accessibility depots or mini grid from small gas turbines or renewable energy sources, like solar, hydro, wind, etc.;

e. Provision of reliable transportation system to connect growth centres, link states and regional centres. The proper functioning of these transportation systems require (i) rehabilitation and expansion of road networks; (ii) improvement and extension of waterway systems in a more economically viable manner; (iii) encouragement of alternative transportation means such as cycles and boats;

f. Production of a long-term plan for railways with a view to providing an East-West rail line in the Niger Delta;

g. The development of water resources and a waste management master plan for the region.

h. The development of standards and procedures for the avoidance of water pollution, especially by collaborating with the oil industry, human waste disposal agencies, etc.

2. Human and Institutional Development

In the areas of human and institutional development, the master plan recommends the:

a. Giving of priority to better education for all people at all levels and the introduction of entrepreneurial skills that are required in productive employment;

b. Collaboration with civil society organisations on initiatives to check and prevent corruption in public places;

c. Re-professionalisation of the civil service in the region through ongoing professional courses;

d. Deliberate efforts aimed at the promotion of merit through building of a detribalised region based on common values rather than differences;

e. Deliberate efforts at integrating governance across the region so that there will be shared ways of pursuing project planning and implementation in the Region.

3. Conflict Resolution and Management

In the area of conflict resolution, the master plan recommends the:

a. Reduction of conflicts by providing efficient security, provision of social services and the improvement of governance;

b. Promotion of core principles and values based on the respect of the rights of others as part of a general principle of conflict resolution;

c. Periodic baseline review of conflict situations in the region so as to translate lessons learned into priority action plan for the region;

d. Establishment in collaboration with other stakeholders of a peace committee for the region;

e. Capacity building for specific groups such as women and youth to facilitate their role in peace-building in the region.

4. Economic Development in Rural Areas

In the area of economic development, the plan recommends:

a. That each state of the Niger Delta should select and execute a demonstrable project in a community or within a cluster of communities,

b. That there should be a Rural Development Service (RDS) for each state with a pool of funds to develop local infrastructure which should facilitate the diversification of local economies;

c. That certain cities, i.e. Port Harcourt, Aba, Warri, Calabar, Benin, Owerri, Akure, Eket, Yenagoa, Brass, should be designated as urban growth poles to serve as centres for development and as catalysts for the development of the Niger Delta.

5. Oil and Gas

In the area of oil and gas, the plan recommends that:

a. Oil and gas should be used to benefit the Niger Delta people by supporting research into areas of manpower needs, industrial markets for the up and downstream oil sectors, etc.;

b. Existing counter-productive policies and programmes within the oil/gas sector should be reviewed;

c. A credible and transparent compensation mechanism for those affected by oil exploration should be defined and established;

d. Steps should be taken to promote the highest level of community participation in decision-making on oil and gas issues affecting localities of exploration;

e. There should be a review of existing environmental policies with a view to strengthening them and ensuring that the impact of oil exploration on the environment is reduced to its barest minimum.

The National Political Reform Conference Report (NPRC), 2005

On February 1, 2005 the President of Nigeria, Olusegun Obasanjo set up the National Political Reform Conference (NPRC) to discuss and to reach a consensus on ways of improving the governance arrangement of the country so that it would reinforce the unity, cohesion, stability, security, progress, development and the performance of the Nigerian Federation. The conference, which had Justice Niki Tobi, a Justice of the Supreme Court, as chairman, had members selected from all states of the federation; elder statesmen, representatives of NGOs, ethnic organisations, the media, social and cultural groups, youths, retired military and police personnel, etc. The recommendations include:

1. The law conferring ownership of land and accompanying resources on the federal government should be reviewed to eliminate corruption and

inefficiency associated with over-centralisation of control over enormous resources and power at the federal government's disposal;

2. The other tiers of government should have greater and more effective say in the development of resources wherever they are located, whilst allowing the federal government to play its regulatory role;

3. There should be a comprehensive compensation package including specified penalties for environmental negligence in the oil and gas sector with a view to bringing it in line with Section 94-97 of the Minerals and Mining Act 1999, which regulates the operations of the solid minerals development sector;

4. States and communities should have a healthy and effective say in the disposal of their resources for there to be development in the region;

5. The problems of the oil-producing communities should remind the country of what the late Sir Ahmadu Bello had to say about the region "…a decay in one part will ultimately affect the rest of the nation. The fate of oil producing communities should be a concern for all";

6. That the right to clean and healthy environment should be enshrined in the constitution as a fundamental human right;

7. That Section 251(1) of the 1999 Constitution should be amended so as to give powers to the states to legislate on matters relating to mines and minerals including oil fields, oil mining, geological surveys and natural gas;

8. The Land Use Act should be reviewed;

9. The various mineral resources of the country should be managed by the federal government through an arrangement with oil-producing states

and communities, and in particular, the rights and privileges conferred on states by the Mining Act, 1999, should be extended to petroleum resources;

10. The issue of derivation should be given greater prominence than presently, in the distribution of the Federation Account;

11. There should be a clear affirmation of the rights of the people of oil-producing communities to actively participate in the management, control and marketing of the resources in their communities;

12. There should be a commission to study, in all ramifications, how the minerals available to the region can best be controlled and managed to the benefit of the people of both the states where the resources are located and the country as a whole;

13. There should be an increment of the derivation from 13% to 17% in the interim, pending the report of the commission, but with a demand by the South-South delegates for 25% with gradual increment to 50% over a five-year period;

14. There should be massive and urgent programmes of infrastructural and human development for the Niger Delta;

15. That bulk allocation should be made to states, irrespective of the number of local government areas in a state;

16. That the derivation principle should be applicable to all accruable revenues except VAT.

UNDP: Niger Delta Human Development Report (UNHDR), 2006

In 2006, the United Nations Development Programme (UNDP), Nigeria, carried out a survey on human development conditions in the Niger Delta as part of an integrated development programme for the region. The report looked at the many dimensions of human development challenges in the region especially as they affect women and youths, and focused on seven key areas. These include:

1. Promotion of peace as the foundation for development;
2. Making local governance effective and responsive to the needs of the people;
3. Improvement and diversification of the economy;
4. Promotion of social inclusion and improved access to social services;
5. Promotion of environmental sustainability to preserve people's sustainable livelihoods;
6. Promotion of an integrated approach to HIV/AIDS; and
7. Pursuit of sustainable partnerships for the advancement of human development.

The report, amongst other things, made the following observations:

1. That the Niger Delta suffers from administrative neglect, crumbling social infrastructure and services, high unemployment, social deprivation, abject poverty, filth and squalour, and endemic conflict;
2. That social and economic deterioration, which has been ignored by policymakers, undercuts enormous

possibilities for development of the country as a whole;

3. That inequities increasingly produce intense and frequent conflicts that threaten Nigeria as a whole, and Africa at large;

4. That the top-down development plans used so far have made little impact on the real lives of people in the Niger Delta and has not changed their perception that development planning is anything more than an imposition by the federal government;

5. That inequities in the allocation of resources from oil and gas and the degradation of the Niger Delta environment by oil spills and gas flares continue to adversely affect human development conditions in the region;

6. That the central control of petroleum resources by the federal government has denied the local people the right to benefit from the land which they own;

7. That corruption, mismanagement, rampant human rights abuses, and poor access to justice and widening human security gap have heightened alienation from government and its structures of authority;

8. That human development deprivations are traceable to asymmetrical planning at the national level, and maladministration and inefficiencies at the state and local government levels;

9. That the numerous armed rebellions have disrupted oil production, attracting international attention and contributed to rising crude oil prices;

10. That government interventions in the region have failed to be human-centred, but more concentrated

on 'developmental artefacts'. This has hampered human-centred progress which would have calmed the restiveness in the region.

The report recommended:

1. A peace agenda, which must include education, easier access to justice and more equitable distribution of resources;

2. Institutionalisation of the practice of accountability, transparency and integrity to guide the flow of development resources at all levels, especially at the local government level;

3. A growth pole strategy that would forge closer links between industries and the production of agricultural and mineral products, and galvanise local economies. From the stock of natural and human resources in the Niger Delta, there are immense opportunities for developing a diversified local economy;

4. Empowerment of socially marginalised groups and individuals, stronger social institutions and infrastructure, and the development of the capacity of existing local groups to enhance their participation and reduce different forms of exclusion;

5. Mainstreaming of environmental sustainability in all development activities should be complemented by: (a) A proactive approach to conserving natural resources to reduce pollution, especially from oil spills and gas flares; (b) Set and achieve adequate targets for clean air and water and soil fertility; (c) Rigorous enforcement of environmental laws and standards;

6.   Strong advocacy, including public awareness campaigns on the multidimensional nature of HIV/AIDS and public enlightenment on risky and harmful traditional practices; state and local governments, NDDC, oil companies, other private sector enterprises, NGOs and donors should collectively improve the quality of and accessibility of health care and HIV/AIDS facilities and equipment, and institute actions to curb the spread of the epidemic;

7.   All levels of government, NDDC, oil companies, organised private sector, civil society organisations and development agencies should work collaboratively on programmes for sustainable development and the attainment of the Millennium Development Goals (MDGs).

Report of the Presidential Council on the Social and Economic Development of the Coastal States of the Niger Delta, 2006

In 2006, President Olusegun Obasanjo, in his search for a lasting solution to the deteriorating security situation in the Niger Delta, created the Presidential Council on the Social and Economic Development of the Coastal States of the Niger Delta. The council, with representatives from the coastal states namely: Bayelsa, Rivers and Delta, was mandated to proactively engage and search for solutions to the problems in the region. In March 2007, the council met to review the general security situation in the region and made recommendations aimed at addressing the situation. They include:

1. Sustained rapprochement and confidence-building through dialogue with the youths and militants of the region;

2. Grant of general amnesty to the militants to encourage most of them to leave the creeks for the city and ensure that they engage in legitimate forms of livelihood;

3. Creation of jobs for the youths to help divert their energies to productive use;

4. Training of youths in semi-skilled and skilled vocational activities, especially in the maritime and oil-related sectors of the economy;

5. Economic empowerment of the people of the region as a measure to facilitate their participation favourably in all areas of human endeavour, especially in the oil and gas sector;

6. Setting up of programmes for rehabilitation and demobilisation of the militants;

7. Utilisation of militants for surveillance duties on oil installations in the creeks of the Niger Delta as already being done under the Global Memorandum of Understanding (GMOU) signed with some communities by oil companies (particularly Shell and Chevron);

8. Increasing the current efforts aimed at social and economic development of the coastal states of the Niger Delta by the federal, state and local governments, including oil companies and various intervention agencies and stakeholders;

9. Provision of good and responsive governance at all levels as this has been the major complaint of the militants who have vowed to kidnap government

officials, their relatives and associates as reprisals for lack of good governance;

10. Funding of youth initiatives for peace in the region by government.

The Ministry of Niger Delta Affairs

The Ministry of Niger Delta Affairs was announced by President Umaru Yar'Adua on 10 September 2008. The Ministry of Niger Delta Affairs was created to formulate and execute plans, programmes and other initiatives as well as coordinate the activities of agencies, communities, donors and other stakeholders involved in the development of the Niger Delta region. Their specific functions include:

- Oversee the implementation of government policies on the development and security of the Niger Delta region.
- Coordinate the formulation of the development plan for the region.
- Formulate policies and programmes for youth mobilisation in the Niger Delta region.
- Advise government on security issues concerning the region.
- Liaise with relevant government, non-government and private sector organisations.
- Formulate and coordinate policies for environmental management.
- Liaise with host communities for the enhancement of the welfare of the people and the development of the region.
- Facilitate sector involvement in the region.

- Plan and supervise programmes on public education/enlightenment.
- Liaise with oil companies operating in the region to ensure environmental protection and pollution control.
- Organise human capacity development as well as skills acquisition programmes for the youths.
- Take adequate measures to ensure peace, stability, and security with a view to enhancing the economic potentials of the area.
- Submit reports periodically to Mr. President on all matters concerning the region.

Technical Committee

In June 2008, the government named Ibrahim Gambari, a Nigerian scholar, diplomat and special adviser to UN Secretary-General Ban Ki-moon, to head the summit steering committee. The choice was presented as a compromise between the government's insistence on keeping the Delta crisis an internal affair and the demands of the Niger Delta ethnic leaders and militants for UN or other international mediation. Until 3 July 2008, President Yar'Adua insisted that the summit was crucial to implementing his administration's policies and promised it would not be another "pointless and diversionary jamboree as some fear."

The road to the summit was strewn with controversy. The dominant view in the region was that the government should abandon the idea and form a committee to pull together the recommendations of those previous reports and present them for action. The second major source of controversy and subsequently opposition concerned who was to steer the process.

Although Gambari's appointment had apparently met the demand for a lead mediator from the UN, it was opposed extensively across the region. Much of this opposition was based on recollections that Gambari, as Nigeria's UN ambassador in 1995, had defended the execution of environmental rights activist Ken Saro-Wiwa and eight other Ogoni by the Abacha dictatorship. Voices from outside the Delta weighed in. The main umbrella labour union, the Nigerian Labour Congress (NLC), argued that Gambari had lost credibility by hurting local sensibilities. The issue, however, went beyond Gambari as an individual. The region's leaders also insisted they could not entrust the committee chairmanship to anyone from the country's major ethnic groups. They demanded a committee headed by, and possibly consisting entirely of, (Niger) Delta people or international mediators. Faced with this opposition, Gambari, who had already laid out a programme for convening the summit within 90 days, withdrew.[47]

The report of the technical committee is best summarised in a paper presented by the chairman in one of the conferences in Port Harcourt.

Being a paper presented by Barrister Ledum Mitee, MOSOP President & Chair of the Defunct Technical Committee on the Niger Delta, at the Port Harcourt International Oil and Gas Conference in June, 2011.

The Technical Committee and its Work

The Niger Delta Technical Committee was inaugurated at a period of hightened tension exacerbated by the frustrations and burning sense of injustice that is pervading the region which found extreme expression

---

47   "International Policy Group, Policy Briefing; Africa Briefing N°60 Abuja/Dakar/Brussels, 30 April 2009 ; Nigeria: Seizing the Moment in the Niger Delta"

in attacks on oil installations, kidnappings and assassinations; the nation was at its tenterhooks.

Against the backdrop of a rich history of disturbing economic shortfalls and broken promises intertwined with devastating environmental damage and conflict, there were heightened expectations of the people as many saw the committee as the last bus stop in the realisation of the resolutions of the problems of the region. Many, however, viewed the work of the committee with great skepticism not because of doubts on the ability of the committee to accomplish its assigned task creditably but whether the report of the committee would not join its predecessors on the shelf.

Perhaps to reassure Nigerians, Vice President Goodluck Jonathan, in his inaugural address in urging members to make "suggestions for government's necessary and urgent action", went on to declare: "On behalf of the government, I want to assure you that your recommendations will not be treated with levity."

In receiving the report of the committee on the 1st of December, 2008, the late President Yar'Adua similarly assured that government would study the report urgently and implement those aspects that it believes would lead to the permanent resolution of the problems of the Niger Delta region. These were the circumstances that the committee set down to work, albeit under considerable challenging circumstances, but with full realisation of the expectations of the nation and the international community.

Some Recommendations

In making the recommendations, the committee proceeded from the premise that whilst the problems of the Niger Delta may be homogenous and exhibit a certain measure of similarity, suggesting the same origin, the region is far from homogenous. Thus, while some of the recommendations are generally applicable, others are targeted at unique challenges of states and communities that constitute the region. The committee also recognised that the importance of the region to the country makes the solution to its problems a national issue with international implications, and as such, its solutions ought to be addressed as a matter of national interest.

Furthermore, the committee noted that past and so far existing efforts to redress the Niger Delta crisis have suffered from want of political will. This has resulted in complete lack of trust necessitating that any genuine attempt at redressing the problem has to be dramatic and seen to be sustained and well resourced.

For these reasons, it is suggested that its key recommendations must not only be implemented but implemented as a package and not in isolation. The committee therefore boxed certain recommendations into a compact with stakeholders that would be committed to support critical short-term changes that are necessary for stemming the decline of the region into a blown conflict zone. The short-term compact which seeks to deliver on visible, measurable outputs which should produce material gains within an 18 month period was to be guided by the principle that the three tiers of government and other stakeholders report on progress in implementation every three months.

The key recommendations include:

Funding Infrastructural Development

The committee recommended the establishment of a Special Niger Delta (Infrastructural) Intervention Fund for the needed urgent massive infrastructural intervention in the region. The fund should receive contributions from oil companies, federal and state governments through the Excess Crude Account, Foreign Exchange Reserve as well as international donor agencies, international pledges, grants and private sector sources.

Communities Stakes in Oil Activities

In order to facilitate a situation where communities would voluntarily protect the assets and operations of oil companies, it was recommended that a framework that allows them to share in the wealth available to each community has to be established. The establishment of Community Trust Funds would pool together resources from compensations, royalties, rents and entitlements directly accruing from relations with oil and gas companies. There is thus the need to institutionalise by law, a Community Trust Fund scheme for oil-producing communities which would allow registered community associations and local groups the opportunity to participate in deciding how the funds are used.

Similarly, it was recommended that power and water supplies from the oil flow stations should be extended to communities within 15 kilometres radius of such stations to ensure that the communities have requisite stakes in the continued operation of such flow stations.

Perhaps it is relevant to add here that the current Petroleum Reform Bill provides an excellent opportunity to work out a framework for taking on board the committee's recommendation on the payment of compensation and rentals to oil-bearing land owners at full economic rates and for oil operators to pay royalties into the Community Trust Funds of not less than $2 per barrel.

It was similarly recommended that by 2010, appropriate regulations should be established to compel oil companies to have insurance bonds against environmental pollution, strengthen independent regulation of oil pollution and work towards an effective EIA mechanism. It was also recommended that enforcement of critical environmental laws be made a national priority whilst fraudulent environmental clean-ups be exposed and prosecuted and gas flaring should cease by December 31st 2008.

Increased Revenue

Allocation accruing from oil and gas revenues to the Niger Delta states was to be increased to 25% within a framework in which the additional funds are dedicated largely to new infrastructure and sustainable development of the region.

Infrastructure

It was recommended, amongst others, that the East-West Road dualisation from Calabar to Lagos with at least one link road per state to the coastline should be fast-tracked to ensure completion by 2010 as well as the commencement of both a coastal road and railway from Calabar to Lagos.

Also recommended was that the federal government should provide immediate funding for full take off of the Federal University of Petroleum Resources in Effurun, Delta State and that PTDF be refocused and re-directed to provide scholarship at all levels to make at least 50% of its beneficiaries to be persons from the Niger Delta.

Disarmament, Demobilisation and Reintegration (DDR)

The committee recommended a DDR process that should begin with some confidence building measures on all sides which include ceasefire on all sides, pull back of troops, credible conditions for amnesty and the setting up of a DDR Commission. It is worthy to note that whilst the amnesty proposed by the committee was a component of an entire DDR process, the current amnesty programme appears to be a stand-alone concept with no attempt to address the root causes of the problems that bred armed militancy in the first place.

Since the announcement of the amnesty for militants, there have been some felt concerns which stem from the fact that in so far as the amnesty focused almost exclusively on militancy without any effort to reflect on the underlying concerns of the people of the region, it certainly would not bring about the desired sustainable peace in the Niger Delta. In so far as the policy would appear to be merely designed to appease militant agitations, it was like giving paracetamol to an ill patient. The policy which is supposedly backed by a nasty budget, which is doubtful if it reflects on the militants themselves, appears not to be well thought out as there were no consultations with critical stakeholders and there were no definite and sustainable post disarmament plans. More importantly, it does appear that it makes the false assumption that 'success' of disarmament of a section of armed militants without any serious efforts at addressing the injustices afflicting the region would by itself translate to peace or the end of militant agitation in the Niger Delta.

There is the crying need therefore to re-appraise the current amnesty offer to a credible negotiated Disarmament, Demobilisation and Reintegration (DDR) programme. There is also the need to structure a process that mops up the still available large amounts of small arms and ammunition and put them or most of them beyond the reach of militants and would-be militants. The process would have to be designed to ensure that where disarmament terminates, demobilisation begins and where demobilisation ends, reintegration commences.

Again, it needs be noted that in the committee's view, although there are international best practices on the key elements of implementation of DDR, the natural starting point should be the setting up of a DDR National Commission or Implementation Committee which should draw membership from amongst others, religious leaders, the civil society, government, ideally a UN observer or technical expert for the international community's buy-in, etc. It would be important that the composition should be such as to capture the confidence of the critical stakeholders.

Youth Employment

As international best practices suggest that it might be counter-productive to target any empowerment programme for only the ex-militants in order not to give the impression that only bad behaviours can attract reward, the Technical Committee recommended the establishment of a direct labour Youth Employment Scheme (YES) in conjunction with the states and local governments that would employ at least 2,000 youths in community work in each of the local governments in the Niger delta.

Security Reform

It also needs to be emphasised that any sustainable peace process in the Niger Delta must take into consideration the committee's recommendation to improve the operational integrity of security forces in the region to a level that assures communities and business organisations of safety without harassment and disruption. This would involve definite steps to eliminate all forms of abuses by security forces and institute proper programmes or reorientation, demilitarisation, retraining and accountability of all security operatives.

Concluding Remarks

In the light of the foregoing, it does not require rocket science or the special expertise of someone who served on the committee to decipher how far the recommendations of the committee have been implemented or not. Whilst we must acknowledge the fact that the implementation of the amnesty programme has greatly reduced the hostilities in the region, to the extent that oil production has increased by over 100% over the figures of the pre-amnesty era, the fact that the increased revenue from oil has not reflected in improved livelihoods or facilities available to the oil bearing communities of the region should be of worrying concern.

National Conference 2014

In 2014, there was a National Conference inaugurated by President Goodluck Jonathan. Although the conference was not specifically about the Niger Delta, there were some resolutions that would have significant impact on the region if implemented, and they include resource control, derivation principle and fiscal federalism.

Some Recommendations of the Conference

i. The conference noted that assigning percentage for the increase in derivation principle, and setting up Special Intervention Funds to address issues of reconstruction and rehabilitation of areas ravaged by insurgency and internal conflicts as well as solid minerals development require some technical details and consideration. The conference therefore recommends that government should set up a Technical Committee to determine the appropriate percentage on the three issues and advise government accordingly.

ii. The conference recommended an increase in the level of derivation from the present 13% to 17% in the interim pending the report of the expert commission. Massive and urgent programmes of development of infrastructure and human resources of the Niger Delta should be embarked upon by the federal government.

iii. It said in determining the formula, the National Assembly should take into account allocation principles especially those of population, equality of states, internal revenue generation, land mass, terrain as well as population density provided that the principle of derivation should be constantly reflected in any approved formula as being not less than 13% of the revenue accruing to the Federation Account directly.

iv. The various mineral resources should be controlled and managed by the government of the federation through an arrangement which involves oil-producing states and communities; in particular, the rights and privileges which the Mineral and Mining

Act of 1999 confers on states, local governments, communities and land owners should equally be extended to the case of petroleum resources.

13

THE PANACEA

The Niger Delta region is our home. It is the home of our species of plants and animals which play a vital force in also shaping the world's weather and climate. Fresh water which flow through the delta region is the source of countless food, fibres, and potential new medicines which could be of benefit to humankind. Unfortunately, the region is facing increasing threats.

The pressures on the Niger Delta environment and ecosystems are numerous and are from myriad and diverse sources. Among the pressures, natural resources – land, water, forests and various animal species are being degraded or lost at alarming rate and at current rates, more than half of the ecosystem may be destroyed or severely damaged in the next 20 years.

The reasons for the magnitude and rate of destruction are many and complex. They include poverty, greed, mismanagement of resources, lack of adequate education and trained personnel, under-development, deforestation, illegal dumping of hazardous wastes, but mostly; the pollution caused by the oil industry thereby making Niger Delta region to be no longer sustainable.

Niger Delta being sustainable in the real sense means that the region can uphold itself. It also means that the trees, fish and other biological species are able to grow and reproduce at rates faster than the actual required just to keep their populations stable. This built-in capacity allows every specie to increase or replace itself. Therefore, this ability to reproduce rather quickly makes it possible to harvest a certain percentage of trees or fish every year without depleting the forest or reducing the fish population below a certain unsustainable base number. Sustainable yield can also be applied to freshwater supplies, land and the ability of natural systems such as the atmosphere or a river to absorb pollutants without being damaged. In contrast, the Niger Delta region is bleeding and the natural environment is suffering in an unprecedented manner from the onslaught of humans. As a result, the daily experience of the ordinary people in the Niger Delta today is that of poverty, disease, oppression, widespread abuse of human rights, structural injustice, large-scale corruption, unemployment, ignorance, violence and the certainty of a short lifespan.

Actually, the underlying thesis of this book focuses on the restoration and preservation of a stable Niger Delta region such that the pollution and conflicts in the Niger Delta have animated and dominated discussions which have engaged the attention of concerned citizens and members of the international community.

There are numerous and interconnected root causes of the Niger Delta conflicts. They range from individual or group volition to structural inequality and injustice. However, the grievances of the oil-bearing communities are centered on some key points, namely:

a) Environmental degradation;

b) Human rights violations;

c) Political marginalisation; and

d) Lack of access to oil wealth produced in the region.

Their demands are as follows:
- Remediation of environmental damage of the region by oil exploration and exploitation;
- their rights to fair share of the oil revenue; and
- sensitivity to their collective oppression as a minority group by Nigeria's ethnic majorities.

The grievances involve three interrelated, but analytically distinct issues.

Firstly, all laws relating to oil exploration and land ownership be reviewed. At the National Political Reforms Conference of July 2005, the delegates of the Niger Delta demanded for the repeal of the Land Use Act and the Petroleum Act. They called for the abrogation and repeal of "all laws that expropriate the rights of the people to control their resources;" fixing deadline for the end of gas flaring in the country and relocation of the headquarters of oil and gas companies to their respective areas of operation in the Niger Delta.

Secondly, the issue of natural resources control should be addressed. Late Ambassador M.T. Mbu has apty advocated that Resource Control simply means that if a product is explored from a particular area, the people of the area should be trusted with the management of such product for the federal family of Nigeria, and that they should also be allowed to keep a portion of the product as long as they can explain why they need it. The portion the people keep, he (Mbu) believed, will make for ecological repair.

Thirdly, appropriate institutional and financial arrangements should be put in place by the Nigerian state and the oil multinationals to compensate the oil-producing communities for the developmental and environmental problems associated with oil exploration and exploitation.

The extraction and production of oil and gas by transnational corporations in collaboration with the Nigerian government has engendered, not just neglect but even denied access of local communities to farmlands and fishing grounds as long stretches of thriving forest and arable lands are cut open to allow for laying of pipelines for transportation of crude oil from flow stations and rigs to export terminals, refineries and reservoirs. In many oil communities in the Niger Delta, the activities of exploration and exploitation have killed fishes and destroyed the ecosystem. These are indications of the suppression of the development of the people.

In his forward on *Niger Delta: Rich Region, Poor People*, a book edited by Monsignor John Wangbu, Senator Francis Ellah opined that the book will guide all well-meaning persons in authority towards the enthronement of Justice, equity and fair-play in the management of the nation through the adoption of a suitable oil policy in Nigeria like those of the advanced progressive democracies, where people enjoy unfettered liberty and their God-given human rights to own and manage their resources as well as pay adequate taxes in order to enable government to develop the whole nation according to the will of Almighty God.

For Dr. Peter O. Odili, a-two tenure governor of Rivers State in the Niger Delta region, "You must identify a problem before you talk of solving it. You cannot talk of building peace, happiness and harmony on injustice. Until you solve the Niger Delta problem and address the gross injustice, you cannot have peace."

The United Nations Declaration on Rights to Development of 1986 recognised that the human person is the central subject in the development process and that such development policy should make the human, the main participant and beneficiary of the development. Moreover, an integrated approach must x-ray the needs of the people of a community and design an all-encompassing strategy to address them. The needs of the people may vary among the different groups in the society- men, women and youth. An integrated approach must also seek to understand the existing coping strategies of the local people to changes in their environment and build on them through policy formulation with adequate participation.

The responsibility that companies have to be ethical goes beyond the value that this brings to their businesses. It has to do with the dignity of the people whose lives the company touches directly or indirectly in its operations. Therefore, must the company engage this community, taking into consideration, social sensibilities and refraining from anything that might upset them? Such positive engagements help the company to identify and address its responsibilities, and in the process, be able to win the friendship of the citizenry of the community. The natural place to begin this is at the basic minimum standards below which it is not permitted to go in the form of Corporate Social Responsibility.

The term Corporate Social Responsibility (CSR) has been coined to define how companies behave in social, environmental and ethical contexts. It is about integrating the issues of the workplace, community and the marketplace into core business strategies. Moreso, it is concerned not only with what companies do with their profits but also how they make the profits. It goes beyond philanthropy and legal compliance to address the ways by which companies manage their economic, social, and environmental impact as well as stakeholder relationships in all key spheres of influence.

To meet the required due diligence obligation, companies would be expected to:

- Establish a human rights policy;
- Integrate the policy as a key factor in decision-making throughout the company management systems;
- Conduct human rights "impact assessments" in order "to understand how existing and proposed activities may affect human rights;" and
- Track and respond to their performance.

Importantly, the responsibility to respect human rights would also require the establishment of effective means for those who believe they have been harmed to bring this to the attention of the government and the company and seek remediation, without prejudice to legal channels available.

Under Nigerian laws, oil wealth which is the bone of contention in the Niger Delta conflict belongs to the federal government; and all oil production operations are structured as joint ventures between the multinationals and the state oil company, with the foreign firms as minority partners. This therefore means that the multinational oil companies are literally business partners with the Nigerian government and not with the local people of the Niger Delta whose oil is in their ancestral home.

In conclusion, let us look at the parable of "Who owns the mango tree?" This is a well-known parable in Ubima, Ikwerre village in (Kelga) Rivers State. There is a fruit-bearing mango tree on the fence between your land and your neighbour's. One day, your neighbour comes and tells you that the mango tree belongs to him. You too tell him it is yours. This results in a heated argument that the question is raised about who planted the tree. To answer the question, everyone around comes to find out that in fact, none of you actually planted the mango tree. To therefore resolve this conflict, various solutions are available:

i.   The first solution is that you win and the other loses. Under this possibility, you could claim the tree using force or threat. You could also pluck the fruits in your neighbour's absence.

ii.   The second possibility is that you lose and the other wins. Under this option, it means you surrender the tree to your neighbour and allow him to have it.

iii.   The third possibility is that you lose and the other loses, i.e. both parties lose. This can happen if anyone of you cuts down the tree.

iv.   The fourth possibility is that you win and the other also wins. This is a win-win solution where both parties feel they have gained. At this juncture, several alternatives are available which includes sharing the fruits.

This book proposes the fourth option for the Niger Delta region and the Federal Government of Nigeria.

INDEX

202

207